SHADOW WORK PUBLISHING

SHADOW WORK
- publishing -

Also by Duncan Ralston

Gristle & Bone (collection)

Salvage (novella)

Wildfire (novella)

Woom (novella)

The Method (novel)

Video Nasties (collection)

Ghostland (novel)

In Every Dark Corner (collection)

Afterlife: Ghostland 2.0 (novel)

The Midwives (novel)

Ghostland: Infinite (novel)

Gross Out (novel)

Ghostland: Ghost Hunter Edition (omnibus)

Try Not to Die: At Ghostland w/ Mark Tullius (gameboook)

Puzzle House (novel)

Pedo Island Bloodbath (novel)

Helloween (novel)

The Summoners: Puzzle House 2 (novel)

CVLT

THE LONELY MOTEL
BOOK THREE

DUNCAN RALSTON

CONTENTS

Awaken

A painting of a father and son hung over the bed when Michael Enhart flicked on the lights in Room 9. The two figures stood below a darkening sky, their backs to the viewer, facing a warmly lit farm in the distance. The man's hand lay on the boy's shoulder in a way that felt subtly menacing. Looking at it gave Enhart the creeps.

Weirder than the painting itself, he was pretty certain it hadn't been hanging there when he'd left the room a few hours ago. It was dogs playing poker or something like that, same as when he'd checked in a few days earlier. Whoever made the swap must've done it while he was out getting the girl.

Enhart didn't like the idea of someone entering the room while he was out. That was why he'd put the DO NOT DISTURB sign on the door handle. He didn't want anybody snooping around, particularly now that he had the girl in the room. In fact, he'd chosen this motel not just for its soundproofed walls —a fact mentioned in an old newspaper article about some poor shmuck kid who'd had his genitals mutilated in one of the rooms with a power tool on prom night—but for its staff's alleged discretion. Everyone in the area seemed to be aware of the sorts of things that went down at the Lonely Motel, and it'd been in the news several times for various nefarious reasons, yet people continued their shady business at the establishment unabated. Their drug deals, their romantic trysts, their pimping, their mafia hits, their rendezvous with "ladies of the night."

Enhart was surprised the building hadn't been forced to close its doors, for all that had happened here over the years.

Now, they were screwing around with his room while he was out. He'd planned all of this down to the most minute detail. To have it spoiled by an illiterate maid or that ancient disco reject with the coke nail at the front desk, swapping paintings for some inexplicable reason... it gave him an anxious feeling he couldn't shake, much like the feeling he got from the painting itself.

He peeked out through the heavy curtains again. No sign of anyone in the rain-dampened parking lot, puddles shimmering with red from the motel's neon sign. Beyond the back lot was a stretch of grass followed by the highway. Headlights zipped past intermittently. It was nearly three in the morning. This late, he didn't expect to see much traffic.

He let the curtain fall back into place as the painting drew his attention again, causing him to notice a detail he'd missed on his first look. Within a wooden pen set further back, closer to the house, a black bull mounted a white cow. *Does that count as interracial?* Enhart wondered with a smirk. *BBC?*

He knew as much about porn as he did about cows, which was just enough to not feel too guilty consuming them once in a while. He liked a good greasy burger when he was on a job. At home, the wife cooked. Boiled chicken and quinoa and Brussel sprouts and all kinds of good-for-you shit with next to no fat and less than zero flavor he'd power down his throat with a grin. He'd always been a big guy. Tall and barrel-chested. Christie-Ann was petite, a former high school gymnast. Since they'd first met, she'd always gotten fixated on some new fad diet to stay healthy, stay fit. And because Enhart had never learned to cook—he'd grown up with Hungry Man TV dinners and frozen, packaged junk his dad had warmed to a barely edible state in the toaster oven or the microwave—it meant he was perpetually on some new fad diet with her.

Just like the every so often he watched porn, eating those burgers on the road made him feel like he was cheating on Chris: he might as well have been fucking a new woman every night, for how she'd react if she found out. Especially now that he was a father. And who knew what kind of crap she'd feed him once the hospital let them bring the baby home? Would they all have to eat the same homemade pablum?

Enhart shook away these thoughts as he looked at the girl handcuffed to the bedposts, below the menacing painting of the father and son watching two cows fucking. He envied her, the way she was now. Unconscious. Unaware. The outside world was filled with so many terrible things. So many choices to be made, the human stink of crowds, inescapable noise and lights, an overload of sensory information bombarding you at every moment of every day.

Too much of everything.

Much too much.

Life was less complex in the place she'd just been.

Simpler.

Choices were limited for her own protection. For the protection of her *community*.

Or so they told her.

Nobody knew much about the cult Enhart had rescued her from, this Children of Dinah. Its leader was elusive, never once caught on camera without his hooded cloak. Its hierarchy, rules and rituals were unknown. Just that much was something of a feat these days, with everything an inquiring mind wanted to know available at their fingertips, with documentaries and podcasts and exposés and Twitter threads. Despite all of that, it somehow remained like one of those ancient Greco-Roman mystery cults. They could've been worshipping Dionysus or some ancient mother goddess or even Cthulhu, for all anyone knew —though the name itself was a biblical reference.

There were rumors, of course. That they sacrificed babies. That they were a front for sex trafficking and forced labor, like NXIVM. That they ate human flesh and engaged in intercourse with children. All of this was somewhat typical blood libel stuff associated with "outsider" religious groups. But the fact that nobody knew much of anything *legitimate* about them was uncanny—practically *supernatural*.

What *was* known was only what their name implied: that they were the spiritual children of the biblical character, Dinah, a victim of rape in the Book of Genesis. Were they all victims of rape, like their namesake? Nobody knew. The three previous members Enhart had deprogrammed had barely spoken a word about the cult's activities. It'd been like they couldn't wait to get free, the deprogramming so easy it had seemed like he'd literally handed them the key to free themselves. They'd refused to share their story,

4

keeping details vague or close to their chests, stating they remembered very little. But the trauma all three of them shared was evident. They'd each had visible scars, as well as mental. Some of them fresh. Whether they were from self-flagellation or abuse, they'd never disclosed.

Even so, during his own surveillance he'd seen nothing more disturbing than the typical "love bombing" session, and a few instances in which someone became angry and was led off for a short duration by two other members, only to return within a few hours or a day later wearing a beatific smile.

Like many cults, they dressed blandly. The Children of Dinah all wore gray flannel outfits during the day and, apparently, gray flannel pajamas at night, though the daytime clothing appeared more functional, with pockets and the like. They farmed, singing vaguely familiar hymns, though Enhart's partner, Bob Ingles, usually a whiz with music, couldn't identify them when Enhart hummed the few tunes he recalled back over the phone. They ate outdoors on a long wooden table under a gazebo roof, though he suspected they only did this in the warmer months. How they recruited, how they worshipped, none of that Enhart could get a handle on.

On the bed, the girl's eyelids fluttered. She would wake soon, and she would demand answers. She would want to know *why*.

Enhart would tell her, *Because you are loved*.

He would say to her, *Because it's a lie, everything you've been told. None of it means a damn thing*.

He would tell her the leader she worshipped—whose Everlasting Love she feared losing more than anything else in her small, uncomplicated world—that he was not at all who she believed him to be.

The man she worshipped was a monster, a *murderer*. Unproven, as yet... but still. These days an accusation was as good as catching him with the bloody knife in his hand.

Enhart would say these things to her with certainty, as *fact*, even though he could no longer be certain he believed them himself. Possibly he never had.

There wasn't much he believed in anymore. Not since the year he turned thirteen.

The only thing that mattered to him now was hanging on for one more forbidden cheeseburger in some all-night diner—much like the Land's End Diner he'd eaten at near the Lonely Motel before driving out to get the girl—with detergent stains on the cutlery, the smell of grease and char permeating everything, Top 40 hits of the 1950s and '60s blasting into his ears through headphones as he silently masticated his food. Petula Clark. Pat Boone. The Beatles. Burger. Fries. Chocolate shake, rattle and roll.

As much as those sloppy diner burgers made him feel like he was cheating on Christie-Ann, they also reminded him of the first night he'd spent on the road all those years ago, driving the dark, lonely stretches of highway and dirt roads in his dad's Buick Riviera, watching the backs of road signs reflecting the red of their taillights in the sideview mirror.

Friday cheat nights reminded him of the last day he'd felt true happiness.

Wouldn't be much more of those nights once the baby came home. Be hard to justify being on the road so much. But what else could he do? He couldn't deprogram cultists from behind a desk. Most of his job was field work, and Bob Ingles was shit in the field. They couldn't exactly swap jobs.

The girl on the bed roused with a sleepy mutter.

Enhart stood up straight as a rod. A performance was about to begin, here in this room. A one-man tour de force he'd acted out countless times in cheap motels just like this one, all across the country.

How many people's eyes had he removed the scales from? Had to be at least thirty by now, maybe as much as thirty-five. In a way, he'd followed in his father's footsteps, much as he'd despised the man.

Room 9 of the Lonely Motel, about half a mile from the international airport, was just another hotel room in a long line of them leading all the way back to the year he'd turned thirteen.

Enhart wondered if he had it in him to lie one more time.

He wondered if he was cut out for this, or if he'd just been fooling himself all these years, if the former cult members he'd successfully deprogrammed had all been flukes and persistence.

He wondered if he'd ever escape from under the shadow of his father.

Before these doubts could fully sink their teeth in, the girl on the bed woke up, and Enhart put on his game face.

GLORIA BLINKED AWAKE, the room swimming into focus around her. She was still dressed in her pajamas, gray and loose and crisp from hanging on the line in the sun. Her feet were bare, the soles always dirty, no matter how hard she washed and pumiced them. To her right stood a cheap particle board nightstand with a digital alarm clock, its big red numbers flashing 12:00—12:00—12:00. Beyond the nightstand an open door led to a dim bathroom, the off-white toilet and tub partly visible, surrounded by grimy yellow wallpaper. Another door—closed—to the right of the bathroom, which she guessed was the closet. A dresser stood near the foot of the bed with a small flat-screen television and remote on it, a black plastic phone and a thick yellow phone book beside that.

A motel room.

Gloria sensed the man's presence before she turned her head to take him in. He stood beside the door in front of a window with its thick scarlet curtains drawn, a large man with sparse, slightly messy dark hair, sad brown eyes and red, pouty lips curled upward in a false smile. The chain on the door was drawn, the deadbolt latched. She tried to withdraw from the man but her wrists were shackled to the bed.

"Where am I?"

Her voice was thick with sleep. The strong chemical stench still lingered in her nostrils. When she licked her chapped lips, she could taste it on her skin.

The man's sad brown eyes expressed sympathy. "You're in the Lonely Motel. Near Buffalo International."

"Buffalo, New York?"

The man nodded, followed by a careful and seemingly calculated pause. "You're safe here," he said.

"What is this? Who are you?"

"Who I am doesn't matter. What matters is that you're safe."

"Why did you bring me here?"

He smiled. "Just to talk."

"To talk," she said, narrowing her gaze.

"That's right."

The man began to move toward her. She cringed away from him again, pulling against the handcuffs,

8

the back of her head bumping the frame of a painting she couldn't quite make out in the reflection on the TV.

"I'm not a pervert," he said, holding up his hands, callused palms outward, with what seemed to be a slightly amused smile. "I'm not going to touch you or anything. This isn't like that."

"Then what is it like?" she snapped.

"Like I said, I just wanna talk. Just you and me, for a little while. Then you can go home."

Home. The word caused a flashback to waking in a panic in her small, hard bed as a strong hand covered her nose and mouth in the dark. The cloth in his hand rough and reeking of the same chemical whose ghost still lingered in her nostrils. Struggling against his hand. The sudden sluggishness. Her thoughts growing soupy.

Then waking here, handcuffed to this bed.

"You *kidnapped* me."

He rubbed the back of his neck sheepishly. "For your own good," he groaned. "You know your mother loves you—"

At the word "mother," Gloria snapped. She yanked on the cuffs, the cold metal digging into her wrists and the meat of her palms below the thumbs. The bedposts thumped against the wall but didn't move much, just enough to make a lot of noise inside the room while she screamed, "*Help! Help me! Hell-llllllp!*"

Then she fell silent, her throat raw, letting her arms hang loose against the cuffs.

The walls were soundproof. Of course, they were. He would have put a gag in her mouth if they were thin. Locked her up in some basement cage or a container in an abandoned shipping yard. This wasn't an amateur she was dealing with. He knew how to handle himself. And his victims.

The man was watching her, seemingly unconcerned by her outburst. He wore a tired look, as if he'd seen it all before.

"We're the only ones on this end of the motel," he said finally. "Walls are thick—cinderblock, the old guy at the desk told me. With the door closed, you wouldn't even hear a power tool running inside. That's what the desk guy said, anyways. Actually, he said 'belt sander.'" Her kidnapper shrugged. "I guess he's heard all the stories, too."

Gloria shot a look at the door, at the latch and chain.

She had to turn this around the only way she knew how. She had to *convince* him.

"Where's my wheelchair?"

He gave her a patient look. "You won't be needing it at the moment."

"Where is it?" she snapped.

"I didn't bring your wheelchair, Savannah."

By sheer force of will she managed to keep the emotions the name stirred from her face. "That's not my name."

"Guess I'm in big trouble," the man said with a grin, clearly not buying it. "What is your name, then? What do they call you, where you live?"

"None of your fucking business."

He smiled briefly. "My name is Michael Enhart. Folks call me Mike, or just Enhart." He touched his chest as he said it, as if to someone who spoke a foreign language or had mental challenges. "I know how this all looks, believe me. More than you can imagine. You think I'm the enemy right now. Some kind of sick psychopath maybe. But honestly, I'm just trying to help. You'll come to understand that, I hope. Eventually."

He smiled again, big and goofy with his thick cherry-red lips. The skin around his eyes creasing.

A genuine smile. Friendly.

He wasn't anything like the man she'd expected him to be. She'd expected cruel eyes and crueler hands. The type of so-called "cult deprogrammer" who used to run rampant in the '70s, beating up Hare Krishnas. A high school dropout with a bad temper and a working knowledge of the Bible. This man looked like a big sad teddy bear, with all the cunning and intelligence of a lost sheep.

No, she told herself. He wasn't stupid. That was what he wanted her to think, to lull her into complacency. She wouldn't allow him to manipulate her into a false sense of security by believing he was dumb.

"My name is Gloria," she said.

"Gloria." He nodded, pooching out his plump lower lip as he leaned against the door and stuffed his hands into the pockets of his baggy chinos. "That's a pretty name. Did he choose that for you?"

She held back her anger. "*She* doesn't choose anything for us. We choose our own names."

"And if there's already a Gloria, what then? You choose a last name?"

"There's only one Gloria. Me. And as you can see," she said, moving her body from the hips up, so her legs remained rigid, "I could really use my wheelchair."

He nodded sympathetically, seeming to consider it. "Well, *Gloria*," he said, playing along with only a whiff of sarcasm, "if you play nicely with me, I promise, I'll get you a wheelchair. Not *your* wheelchair— that's three-hundred miles southeast of us. But a chair with wheels, you'll have it. For now, let's just you and me get comfortable where we are. Get to know each other."

She rattled the cuffs. "Hard to get *comfortable* when you're chained to a bed."

"We'll come to that. Soon. I promise you, I'll let you out of those cuffs just as soon as we understand each other."

"I don't think you have the capacity to understand me. I have the Light within me. I carry Her Grace in my heart. You? You're just a sad, lonely old man."

"Two strikes. I'm not old." Enhart raised his left hand, indicating his wedding ring. "*And* I'm not lonely. I got a wife waiting for me at home."

"That ring doesn't mean you're not lonely."

He shook his head with a tight smile, holding her gaze. "You don't know me."

"I know your kind."

He touched his chest, looked around with a playful grin. "My *kind*? I told you, I'm no psycho, Gloria. I'm a friend of your mother's."

"She's *not* my mother."

"Well, then I'm a friend of the woman who gave birth to you. Is that fair?"

"Dinah gave birth to me. She pushed me from Her celestial womb into a world of darkness and despair, where I flailed and floundered until I rediscovered Her Truth and Her Way."

The man smiled. Glanced at the painting.

"Let me out," she said.

"You ever wonder if your God is a practical joker?"

She didn't reply.

"I wonder sometimes..." he said, and let the thought linger. It seemed like he was musing, going off-script, but she doubted it. Not this early. He was a conman. A grifter. A charlatan working his marks. He'd have standard patter, things he said to all of his victims. "If we were made in God's image, why do we so often turn our hearts toward the darkness?"

The comment surprised her. "She gave us free will. Let me out."

"I will let you out, Gloria. But first, as I said, you and I have to come to an understanding."

She narrowed her gaze. Finally, he was making his play. "What kind of understanding?"

"I want you to know I'm trying to help you. I want you to *believe* it."

"You really want to *help* me? Take me back to my family."

"That's my intention. Your muh—" He stopped himself, clearly about to repeat his earlier mistake. "The woman who hired me, who happens to share your last name and possesses your birth certificate, as well as plenty of photos of you as a kid—which she sent me copies of, by the way—she paid me a not-in-significant amount of money to bring you home."

"That's *not* my home."

The light smile again. "Okay. You're an adult, you can make your own decisions. But I'm betting you don't make a lot of decisions where you live right now, do you, Gloria?"

He eyed her for an uncomfortably long time. She held his gaze as long as she could, willing him to break first, to look away. When he didn't, she glanced toward the ceiling, catching just the bottom of the framed painting above her head. He looked at it again and the troubled look from before returned for only a moment.

"Show me the painting," she said. "You keep looking at it. I wanna know why."

He scowled briefly. "I'd have to take it down."

"Would you? As a..." She considered her words. "...a gesture of peace."

"Gesture of peace, huh?" He nodded with a shrug. "All right."

The man—Michael Enhart, he'd called himself, Mike or just Enhart—moved toward her from his place near the windows. She cowered as he approached the bed, despite this being her idea. He gave her another glimpse of his callused palms with that same sad smile, then leaned over her. She could hit him if she wanted to. Headbutt him in the groin or grab the folds of his belly and squeeze. But that was against Dinah's plan for her. The man would overpower her quickly. Besides, there was no point doing anything until she was able to get him to uncuff her from these bedposts.

So, she rested her head against the headboard while he removed the painting from the wall, his shirt coming untucked to expose his hairy, bulging white belly.

He stepped back with the painting in hand, then spun it around for her to see. It was a landscape of a father and son and farmhouse with two cows rutting in the background, all under a cloud-covered sky minutes before sundown. What Hollywood used to call the "magic hour." The artwork was competent and there was something tragic about it that Gloria couldn't quite put her finger on. Maybe it was the way the father's hand seemed to squeeze the boy's shoulder, as if forcing him to stay put.

Were the father and son watching the cows rut? Was the father imparting some kind of lesson, some wisdom? Gloria didn't know, but it seemed the painting spoke of generational pain, something she understood deeply. She looked up at the man holding it. He appeared to be trying to gauge her expression.

She could see why it bothered him.

"What does it say to you?" she asked.

He glanced down at it, obviously unable to see it well from above. With a shrug, he said, "Not much."

She frowned. "If you want us to understand each other, you're going to have to stop lying to me."

Again, he shrugged. "I don't know what it *says*, but it makes me feel..." He licked his lips. "...uncomfortable, I guess. It makes me think of that old song, you know?" He sang his next words lightly: "*How ya gonna keep em down on the farm, after they've seen Paree?*"

"You have a nice voice," she said, not lying.

Enhart scowled. He hung the painting back on the wall, and gave it a slight look of distaste before stepping back and looking down at her. "Buttering me up isn't going to help us reach that understanding, Gloria."

"Then what *will* help? What can I do to convince you to *let me go*?"

"You can start by telling me the truth."

"About what? You *kidnapped* me from my room in the middle of the night—"

"I wanna know about the people you live with. Your so-called *family*." He spoke this last word with obvious disdain. "I want you to tell me everything you know about the Children of Dinah. Once you've told me that, then maybe we can talk about letting you out of this room."

She narrowed her eyes in suspicion. "You want me to talk about my friends. That's it?"

He half-nodded. "That's it."

"Then you'll let me go?"

He waited a moment before saying, "If I'm satisfied with what you tell me, I'll let you go back home."

"Which home?"

"You know which home, Gloria."

"Then what's in it for me? My home is with my family. With the other Children."

"I can't take you back there. But if that's where you *choose* to go after all is said and done..." He shrugged. "I can't *make* you stay with your moth—the woman who raised you."

Gloria considered her next words carefully. "Okay. How about this... how about we make a deal?"

"I'm not interested in deals, Gloria."

"Please," she begged. "Just hear me out."

He crossed his arms. For a moment she thought he wouldn't allow it, and even if he did let her go on, he wouldn't *truly* listen. Then he nodded for her to continue.

"How about... if I can make you believe in three miracles—I'm talking honest-to-God, hand-on-heart miracles—you let me go back with my family. Not the woman who paid you to bring me here. My *real* family, Michael."

"Three miracles, huh?" He chuckled, uncrossing his arms. "And here it's not even Christmas."

"I'm serious."

He glowered at this, his puppy-dog features replaced by a flat expression, hinting at a brute, cold cruelty beneath. "I don't believe in miracles, Gloria."

"Neither did I," she said. "Not until I met my brothers and sisters."

Enhart shook his head in obvious disbelief. "If you can get me to believe in *one* miracle, that's miracle in itself. But okay. Three miracles." He grinned. "I'd say you got your work cut out for you, but you probably already know that."

"Okay. Thank you. Then I guess I should start with the first," she said, and with that she began to tell the story, one she knew by heart. "They said she was—"

POSSESSED

T hat's what her priest and parents decided, anyway. This bright-eyed little girl, vibrant and precocious, taken by the Devil just weeks before her confirmation. Her name was Chloe and she was just twelve years old.

Chloe's parents tried everything they knew. This was the Sixties, and little girls just didn't behave the way she'd been. Spare the rod and spoil the child, they used to say, so the mother and father tried spanking her to get her to straighten up, and when that didn't work, they whipped her with belts and hairbrushes. They tried washing out her mouth with soap, and locking her in her bedroom closet with nothing to eat for dinner. They tried cold neglect. They tried prayer. None of it worked.

She'd been a star pupil in Father Epsilon's Sunday school classes, and an alto in the church choir. She'd always been a good girl, an A-student and the perfect child. But then she'd started crying at odd times, particularly when it came time to have her baths. Her mother had to practically force her to brush her hair and teeth. Just getting her to change her clothes for school was a chore. She even stopped wanting to play with her friends, where before they had trouble getting her to come home for dinner.

Worse, she'd wake up screaming all kinds of gibberish in the middle of the night, words that didn't even make sense together. Word salad, her dad called it. Soon she started coming home from school with deep scratches on her arms and legs, which at first they'd thought were inflicted by another student, but quickly realized, when they noticed dried blood and flecks of skin under her own fingernails, that she'd been doing it to herself.

The scars were easy enough to hide, and she never acted out in public. Actually, she was very shy and withdrawn when they took her to church or school or events with family and friends. She'd always been polite, never talking the ears off of adults the way some parents let their kids do—mother and father were still of the "children should be seen and not heard" generation, though they were a little more lax about it than their own parents had been. Now, they could barely get her to speak if they tried.

The absolute worst, the most embarrassing part by far for Mom and Dad, was the day she got sent home for drawing a monster with a huge cock in her school notebook. And not just one of them. It was *all over* the book, in various positions and states of arousal. Cocks dripping semen, spewing it like a fountain, flaccid and droopy, hard and pointing upward like a dowsing rod.

Her teacher asked them, as delicately as possible, where Chloe might've gotten these ideas. Teachers just didn't talk about those things in class, and parents in those days sure didn't have those conversations with their kids. Even those that might would never get that graphic. They'd only just started to teach sex ed in some schools but those were *city* schools, in progressive areas, and in Chloe's school and grade, in their white-picket-fence neighborhood in their small town in 1969, they were very far from progressive.

Chloe's parents didn't have any idea. She must've gotten it from one of the other kids, but who would raise their children to know such things and share them with innocent little girls? What sort of child would *behave* like that?

It was Dad, later on that night, who noticed the monster looked a bit like a demon, complete with tiny horns. And in some of the drawings, the demon had its hand on the shoulder of a little girl in a blue dress. In others, it *seemed* to be leaning down to whisper in her ear.

The idea seized hold of Chloe's folks, and they discussed it the following evening after dinner while the little girl was upstairs doing her homework. The following Sunday, they had to practically wrangle her to go to church. She threw a tantrum in the backseat of the car, and they decided Mom should stay home with her. If anyone asked, Dad would say they were sick with the flu and didn't want to spread it around. Considering how badly behaved she'd been the previous Sunday, nobody asked.

Once the service was over, Dad showed the notebook to Father Amos Epsilon. Father Epsilon was gravely concerned. He suggested they perform an exorcism at once.

Reluctantly, Dad agreed.

Monday evening, after another dinner which the little girl spent in her bedroom with nothing to eat, Father Epsilon came to their door with a man dressed all in black, like the priest himself. Only this man wasn't wearing vestments and a white collar. He wore a black coat, vest and pants with a white dress shirt. Mom remarked later that he looked a bit like Johnny Cash, though his slicked hair was slate gray and thick-rimmed glasses rested on his bulbous nose, the lenses tinted a slight orange. His cheeks and prominent chin were pockmarked with pimple scars.

"I'm Paul Petrichor," the man said, holding out his right hand to shake. He held a leather satchel like a doctor in the left. "I'm the exorcist."

"Glad to meetcha," Dad said, shaking his hand.

"Likewise," the exorcist said.

"Pleasure to meet you," Mom said, and when Paul Petrichor took her hand, rather than shake it he bowed slightly and raised it to his lips to give it a kiss, holding her gaze.

"The pleasure is mine. All mine."

Mom blushed.

Petrichor looked into the dining room, at the table set for two. "Where's the girl?"

"Chloe's in her room," Dad said. Mom was still flustered and a bit embarrassed.

Father Epsilon gazed down at his shoes.

"Listen, you're going to hear a lot of strange noises coming from up there," the exorcist told them. "She may scream bloody murder. It may *seem* like she's in imminent peril. But she'll be fine, I promise you that. Children are very resilient. The only *peril* she's in is her immortal soul. So please... whatever you hear, whatever you *think*, you *mustn't* enter her bedroom under *any* circumstance. If you disturb Father Amos and I during the exorcism, the *demon* inside of her will *seize* that opportunity—" He made claws with his fingers. "—to *claw* its way *deeper* into her *soul*—" He dragged his fingers toward himself. "—and from that, she may *never* come back."

Mom gasped.

"You want your little girl back, don't you?"

Both Mom and Dad agreed vehemently that they wanted their little girl back.

"Then for God's sake, whatever you do, *do not open that door* once Father Amos and I have stepped inside."

Mom and Dad agreed that they wouldn't go into her room, no matter what.

"Good. When we come back down those stairs," the exorcist said, "we'll have your demon. Right, Padre?"

Father Epsilon looked up from his shoes and nodded briskly. "That's right, Paul."

"What do we do? While you're performing the..." Dad couldn't bring himself to say the word *exorcism*. "The ritual," he said instead. "Father Petrichor," he added hastily, ever the good Catholic boy.

"Call me Paul, please. I'm no priest."

"You're not?"

"No, sir," the exorcist said. "What I am is a spiritual vessel, skilled in the removal of demonic possessions from twelve different religions. I have studied the Bible, the Torah and the Talmud, the Koran, the Bhagavad Gita *and* the Book of Mormon," he emphasized, as if this latest holy book was slightly more impressive than the rest.

"Well, it sounds like you're quite experienced," Mom said.

"That I am," the exorcist said, returning his wolfish gaze to her. "I have performed over a hundred successful exorcisms and several *ruqya*, the Islamic practice for removing genies."

"Genies?" Dad asked skeptically. "Like the blonde on the boob tube?"

Mom blushed again. Dad always called it the "boob tube," but he seemed to emphasize the *boob* part a little more when talking about *I Dream of Jeannie*.

The exorcist gave him a patient smile. "*True* genies of the Muslim faith are *nothing* like Barbara Eden," he said. "In actual fact, they make the djinn of *The Arabian Nights* look like lapdogs! Believe you me, you do *not* want to come face to face with one of those heinous devils."

Dad chuckled anxiously. "No, I wouldn't imagine," he said.

So, Mom and Dad took Father Epsilon and the exorcist up to Chloe's room, where she was sitting cross-legged on the floor when they opened the door. She didn't look up from her book.

"Honey, Father Epsilon is here," Mom said.

Still not looking up from her homework, Chloe said, "I know," sullenly.

"Honey, be polite."

Finally, Chloe looked up, lifting her big, sad blue eyes to the men in the doorway before raising her head. "Hello, Father Amos. Hello, Paul."

"What have we said about addressing adults?" Dad scolded her, wondering how she knew to call him Paul in the first place. He figured she must've been listening through the heat vent to their conversation in the foyer.

"Hello, Mr. Petrichor," she said, and her eyes slid from the priest to him, unblinking.

"Hello, demon," the exorcist said.

The little girl said nothing.

Petrichor reached into his bag. He pulled out a

large wooden crucifix, the size of the one over the fire-place downstairs, and held it up to Chloe. "Foul beast, leave this poor girl's soul *this instant*, in the *name* of Jesus Christ Our Lord, amen!"

"Amen," Father Epsilon said belatedly.

"Can I have dinner now?" Chloe asked her mother with a pout.

Petrichor glanced back at her parents. "This is going to be tougher than I thought. The demon isn't responding to traditional Christian symbols. It may be rooted deeper than you first suspected, Father Epsilon."

Father Epsilon nodded gravely. "Yes, I do believe you're right, Paul."

"All right, folks. It's time for the padre and I to do our work," the exorcist said, ushering them to the door. Mom and Dad glanced at their daughter, reluc-tant to leave her but knowing it was their only choice.

They'd tried everything they knew how to get their little girl back. These men were their last resort.

So they left the room, and Paul Petrichor closed and locked the door behind them. In the hall they gave each other a nervous look. Dad sighed and put a hand on Mom's shoulder. Soothed slightly, she made her way back downstairs. Dad followed her.

Over the next hour they heard whimpers and weeping. Thumps on the floor. Something rattling. The priest cried out several times, and Petrichor bel-lowed, the words of his prayers and incantations muf-fled. He could've been screaming heresies for all they knew, Dad with his feet up in his recliner, smoking his pipe while trying to read the paper, Mom darning sev-eral pairs of his black dress socks on the sofa, while the zany cast of *The Carol Burnett Show* tried not to laugh at Tim Conway's shenanigans on the TV.

At one point a sudden loud thump followed immediately by a violent shout from Petrichor startled Dad so badly he jumped up in his recliner. A smoldering clump of tobacco flew out of his pipe and landed on his shirt. He brushed it off with a flurry of embers and stamped it out on the floor. Mom and Dad both looked up from the soot ground into the carpet and gave each other an anxious look. But neither of them seemed to be able to express how worried they were that their priest, a pious yet gentle man, had brought a grifter into their home.

They'd pulled their daughter from school the entire week, telling the principal she had the mumps, and this routine continued for several days, night after night. Dad would return home from work. They'd eat supper, just the two of them, since their little girl was on a "spiritual fast," according to Petrichor, to help rid her of the demon. ("You know what they say, honey," Dad said jokingly one night, as Mom returned a third plate to the china hutch, "feed a fever, starve a possession," and the two of them chuckled anxiously.) Shortly after supper, the two men would arrive, the exorcist with his bag of tricks, Father Epsilon staring at his shoes rather than being his usual talkative self. Every night, after the men left, she'd beg Mom and Dad to let her go, but Petrichor had warned them about this very thing. He'd said she'd try to suck up to them, to be sweet and kind and seem and sound exactly as if God had seen fit to return their little girl to them. So, despite their reservations, they persevered, because they trusted their priest completely. He'd been their spiritual leader for as long as the two of them could remember. He'd baptized their little girl, after all. And Father Epsilon trusted the exorcist.

So they told her what they were doing was for her

own good, that she'd be happy they did this when all was said and done. Then they'd tell her good night, that they loved her, and she'd spend the next several hours weeping, which they heard from their bedroom next door while they lay in their own bed, each of them wondering, but not daring to broach the subject, if what they were doing was wrong. If it wasn't, actually, against God's will.

On the sixth night, Mom slammed her cutlery down on the table and looked at her husband plainly. "I can't do this anymore. It's been almost a week. They've been up there, doing God knows what—"

"Honey," Dad said.

Mom thought he'd try to stop her from saying what she needed to say, to tell her it was hubris to think she knew more than a man of God, or worse, that she was acting hysterical. They were both religious, but they weren't exactly *devout*. They went to church every Sunday, they fed the collection plate and did Communion and sang along with the hymns just like everyone else, but they didn't pray before bed anymore, and they'd each caught each other taking the Lord's name in vain once or twice.

When it came to matters of religion, Mom had always been the one to make decisions for the household. Why change that now?

Instead, Dad said, "You're right. We've got to put a stop to it. This can't go on forever. She'll starve—"

"She won't starve."

Dad frowned and laid down his fork. "What do you mean? She hasn't eaten anything in six days."

"I've been giving her soup and a handful of saltines at noon," Mom said.

"But we promised Father Epsilon—"

"We *promised* Paul Petrichor. And that man... I

don't know about you but he doesn't exactly inspire the faith Father Epsilon does. I think..." Mom leaned over the table and added in a whisper, "I think he might be a *conman*."

"I thought the same thing," Dad said, pushing around his mashed potatoes. "Father Epsilon's a good man. But I think his faith might've blinded him to the exorcist's more... *unsavory* qualities."

Mom blushed again, having endured the exorcist's leering looks since he'd first set foot in their door.

"Petrichor's the problem," Dad decided. "If Father Amos says our little girl's possessed, I believe him. I just don't believe this exorcist's a spiritual vessel at all. I don't even think he *believes in God*—at least not the same one we pray to."

"I think you're right," Mom said. "You heard the way he talked about genies. What if he's—" She dropped her voice even lower, hunching over her roast beef. "—*a Mohammedan?*"

Dad wiped his lips in disgust and threw his napkin on the table.

The two of them decided they'd tell Father Epsilon tonight was the last night. If they didn't rid their little girl of her possession, they'd live with it. The way she'd been acting night after night as they put her to bed... well, maybe she *hadn't* been faking. Maybe the demon had escaped while the men weren't watching, and they'd been shouting their rites at a poor, confused twelve-year-old.

"One more night," Petrichor promised them, sharing a nervous look with Father Epsilon at their front door. "As Jesus cast Legion into the *herd of swine*, I promise you, I *solemnly swear*," he said with a hand on the breast of his suit jacket, "by *His* power and *His* name, Father Amos and I will *rid* your little girl of this *demonic plague* before the clock strikes midnight."

Mom and Dad shared an anxious look themselves. Dad nodded. Mom agreed. "One more night," they said in unison.

"Remember," the exorcist said, "*whatever* you hear, *whatever* you *think, do not* go upstairs. That's more important tonight than ever."

"We won't," they both said, the way they said "Amen," in church after Father Epsilon raised the Host and said, "The body of Christ."

But they had no intention of obeying. They'd planned to creep upstairs while the two men were absorbed in the rites and make sure Petrichor's faith was up to snuff. What if the only demon in this house was led here unintentionally by their own priest? What if the only devil was using God's own tools—the crucifix, the holy water and the Bible—against an innocent little girl?

About an hour into the chants, the bellows, the sudden thumps, Dad put down the paper he hadn't really been reading and sat his unlit pipe on the table beside his recliner. Mom set the underpants she'd been darning and her sewing kit aside, and the two of them crept to the stairs and listened.

"From *plague*, from *famine*, from *war*!" Petrichor bellowed, punctuating each word with a grunt, as if he was splashing her with holy water or thrusting the crucifix at her with all the fury of the Almighty.

"Deliver us, O, Lord," Father Epsilon almost seemed to pant.

Dad nodded at Mom. Mom returned the nod, and the two of them began creeping up the stairs.

"From *ever! Lasting! Death!*"

"Deliver us, O, Lord."

Halfway up the stairs, a step creaked under Dad's foot. He paused, wincing at the sound. Mom gave him a stern glare.

They watched Chloe's door through the second-floor railing, the light beneath bustling with shadows, waiting for those shadows to open the door and catch them on the stairs.

But Petrichor's exorcism continued unabated, so Mom and Dad kept ascending.

"By the *mystery!* Of your *holy! Incarnationnnnn!*"

"Deliver us, O, Lord."

On the second floor now, they crept toward Chloe's room. Up here they were just able to hear the muffled sound of Chloe's whimpers, as if they'd covered her mouth. It made Mom and Dad quicken their step, even while creeping quieter than ever.

"By your *coming!*" Petrichor bellowed.

Another muffled whimper.

"Deliver us, O, Lord," Father Epsilon pleaded.

They reached her door. The gathered shadows writhing in the light at their feet sent a chill up their spines. Something *evil* was in that room, of that they had no doubt. Whether it was an unholy evil possessing their daughter or a shrewder, manmade evil, they didn't yet know. But they were eager to find out.

"By your *birth-ah!*" Petrichor shouted, starting to sound like some tent revival Baptist preacher.

"Deliver us, O, Lord!"

Dad put a finger to his lips and slipped the key into the lock.

"By your *baptism-ah!* And your *holy! Fasting-ah!*"

Dad turned the key. The sharp click made them both cringe in the dim light of the second-floor hall, but the exorcist and the priest were fully absorbed in the rites, and didn't seem to hear them.

"Deliiiiiiver us!" Father Epsilon cried. "Oh! *Oh! Oh, Lord!*"

"By your *cross-ah!*" Petrichor shouted. "And your *passion-ah!*"

Rather than chant his "deliver us," Father Epsilon howled in holy fervor.

Dad pushed open the door with the slightest of creaks.

What they saw caused his jaw to drop. Mom shrieked and clutched her pearls.

The priest and the exorcist had their precious little girl *pinned* to the bed, Father Epsilon filling her mouth, the exorcist fuck—

"*JESUS FUCKING CHRIST!*" Enhart said, holding up both hands in disgust. "I don't need to hear this."

Gloria smirked. "Weak stomach, Michael?"

"I just don't wanna hear graphic details about *child rape*, all right? It's *horrible*." He didn't want to tell her he was about to be a father to a girl himself. That if he'd caught someone abusing his little Jessa— that was the name Christie-Ann had chosen for her, and Joshua if it was a boy—he'd tear them apart with his bare hands, pacifism be damned.

"If you think it's bad hearing about it, imagine what it was like for that poor little girl," Gloria said.

Enhart held her challenging gaze for a long moment. "This story isn't about you, is it?"

"Do I look like I was born in the Sixties?"

"No, I guess not."

"This is a part of our gospel, Michael. The First Survivor is our spiritual leader. From Her suffering and rebirth arose a movement, more powerful and transformative than any that came before it."

"You know how many times I've heard that, in one cheap motel after another?"

She gave him a shrewd look. "How many?"

He shrugged. "I can't count. Rough estimate: thirty? Forty?"

Gloria closed her eyes and nodded lightly. When she opened them again, she asked, "Do you know the story of Dinah? From the Bible?"

Enhart nodded. "Of course, I do. Wouldn't be very good at my job if I hadn't studied the Bible front to back, would I?"

"I don't know. Some of you deprogrammers, I hear you get off on the violence. Brute strength and sadism, those are the tools of your trade. You like the power."

Enhart shook his head, swallowing a bitter taste. He knew exactly the type of man she was talking about, and he'd done everything in his power *not* to be like him. "Yeah, well I'm not that guy."

"No?"

He crossed his arms, then quickly uncrossed them, realizing a moment too late how defensive it made him look, and how silly the overcorrection would seem. The story of Chloe and her exorcist had shaken him, he had to admit. Had that been her plan? He didn't know. What he did know was that this woman—barely older than a girl herself—was more clever than many of the jobs before her. She'd caught his negative reaction to the father-and-son painting, when he thought he'd been careful. He'd need to be far more vigilant with his body language and words if he wanted to win her over to the good side. "No," he responded.

Gloria held his gaze in silence a moment longer. Then she said, "So you know how Dinah got revenge on her rapist."

"Sure. Jacob, her dad, told his sons, Simeon and Levi, to go into town and trick the prince who raped her into convincing all the men there to get circumcised so they could marry into Jacob's family. And while the men were still recovering from their snipped tips, Simeon and Levi returned to town and killed every last one of em. Only they didn't stop there: they stole their livestock, took everything of value from their homes, they even kidnapped their wives and mothers and children."

"Exactly," Gloria said, her eyes practically sparkling. "The best revenge isn't to be unlike your enemy. It isn't living well. The best revenge is *revenge*. Coldblooded. Calculated. Forget about an eye for an eye. If someone takes your eye, you take the eyes of their family, their friends, their pets. And you *leave* your enemy their eyes to *witness it*."

Enhart blew out a breath in surprise. "I guess the Children of Dinah aren't big on turning the other cheek."

Gloria scoffed. "Neither was Jesus. He wasn't some hippie philosopher. He said a lot of dark shit, and you don't even have to look at the New Testament closely to find it. In Matthew, He condemns people who commit evil acts to a *blazing furnace*, meaning Hell. That sounds a lot like *an eye for an eye* to me. Actually, it sounds like *more* than an eye for an eye. He told his disciples that Sodom and Gomorrah got better treatment from His Father than the towns who rejected His gospel should get from them. He literally *bans* people from entering the Kingdom of

Heaven unless we *believeth in Him*. What's so kind and forgiving about that?"

"Well, when you put it that way...."

"Right. Jesus was a hypocrite. And the *worst kind*. He was a *self-righteous* hypocrite."

Enhart shrugged. He wasn't religious himself— *lapsed*, if he had to define it—and blasphemy was often part of his repertoire when working with members of Christian-flavored cults. "I guess that's up for interpretation," he said.

"Only if you cherry pick," she snapped back.

"Well, that's it, isn't it? There's a lot to cherry pick from, whether you're a holier-than-thou born-again or a loudmouth atheist. It's a long, complex book with a lot of ideas crammed into those pages. It's also a couple thousand years old."

"The original texts are. What we have now was memorized and reinterpreted by monks in the Middle Ages. It's a game of broken telephone with God and the apostles on one end and a bunch of drunk incels on the other."

Enhart laughed. "Aren't incels *in*voluntarily celibate? It's right there in the name."

She gave him a smug look. "You really think a guy who could get laid in those days was lining up for vows of silence and chastity?"

"Some," he said, shrugging. "You never see a good-looking priest before? Or an attractive nun?"

With a chuckle, Gloria said, "Did you know the paranormal investigators or so-called 'demonologists,' Ed and Lorraine Warren, had an underage girl living with them as a sex toy? Ed was fucking her and his wife Lorraine knew all about it."

"I didn't know that."

"It's true. They're a billion-dollar industry now. You ever see the *Conjuring* movies? Or *Amityville*?"

"I'm not really a horror fan."

"Well, they say they're based on true stories, but none of that supernatural stuff is real. We all know there's no devil. No demons." She shook her head. "True evil is born in the hearts of men."

"And women," Enhart added, a little too quickly.

Gloria smirked. "Yes, and women."

The silence held for a moment. Aside from the occasional motorcycle or tractor trailer on the highway, Enhart hadn't heard anything beyond these walls. As if the walls didn't just block sound but *absorbed* it. Either the soundproofing the old guy at the desk mentioned was better than in any motel he'd ever stayed at before, or the entire place was empty.

The guy did say the whole motel was empty except for one couple, he remembered. *Said this was the quietest room in the place, except for that one.*

Enhart had thought that was weird in itself. A no-tell motel like this, there'd usually be hookers and johns going in and out, at the very least, with pimps or cabs picking them up. Squeaky bedframes, grunts and groans. People leaving their rooms to use the ice machine. Others to have a cigarette.

The Lonely Motel had none of this. It was almost spookily quiet. As if, aside from the vehicles passing by in the distance, there was only the two of them in this room enclosed in their own little pocket universe.

He had to forcibly prevent himself from shuddering.

WRATH

"What happened to Chloe?" Enhart asked finally, if only to break the oppressive silence. "After the parents found out."

"What do you think happened?"

"Well, I'm guessing the poor kid was acting out because the priest'd been abusing her after Sunday school or choir practice."

"He was."

Enhart nodded thoughtfully. "So I *hope* that her parents called the cops on em. Her abusers went to jail for a very long time, Chloe got counselling and grew up well-adjusted, aside from some very understandable issues trusting new men in her life."

Gloria blinked at him.

"But since you said she was the First Survivor," he went on, "and considering you mentioned Dinah's revenge against her abuser and the men who enabled him... I'm guessing it didn't turn out that way."

"Look at you, Veronica Mars," she said, impressed. "No, it didn't turn out that way at all. This isn't a story about forgiveness, Michael. This is about *wrath*."

Enhart nodded somberly. "I guess things didn't turn out so hot for Father Epsilon and the exorcist, then."

"Not so much. I need to pee," she said, and waggled her fingers in the cuffs, pouting slightly. "Please?"

Enhart eyed her suspiciously. "How do I know I can trust you?"

"It's not like I can run away, can I?"

Enhart glanced at her legs. He'd been consciously trying not to look at them, hoping to not make her self-conscious about it. He knew she required a wheelchair. Her mother had told him on the phone about the accident in her late teens, and even if she hadn't, he'd seen Savannah or Gloria as she called herself now using it at the commune. He'd thought about how difficult and cumbersome it must've been for her on the dirt paths, bending down to garden along with the others appeared difficult for her, and he could only imagine how hard it must be to do chores around the big house.

He'd thought about taking it with them, but rolling her out in a squeaky wheelchair wasn't exactly conducive to sneaking out of the Children of Dinah compound in the dead of night, and it wasn't like he could run back in to get it after having just fireman-carried an unconscious young woman out to his car.

So he'd left it.

And now she needed to use the bathroom.

"Well, can you hold it?" he said anxiously.

Her eyes flashed with annoyance. "I've *been* holding it since I woke up. I need to go, Michael. *Please*."

Enhart waffled. He wasn't at all worried about her attacking him or running away. He was anxious about having to get her on and off of the toilet.

36

The thought of having to take off her pants and possibly her panties for her, or holding her up while she took them off herself, and then lowering her half naked down to the toilet seat... it made him think of those illicit cheeseburgers in the all-night diners with the little jukeboxes on the tables. It made him think about the porn films he watched once in a while, on nights he'd come back exhausted from doing recon at one cult or another, if the motel had the channels unlocked and he couldn't get to sleep.

He sighed heavily. "All right," he said, approaching the bed. "You try anything, it's gonna be a bad night for you locked up in that closet."

She smirked. "I thought you didn't get off on violence."

Scowling, he said, "It's not violence. It's a time-out."

She shrugged. "Whatever helps you sleep at night."

Enhart exhaled through his nostrils. "Do you want me to take you to the bathroom, or would you rather piss the bed?"

"Bathroom." She rattled the handcuffs again, looking up at him with her dark, downturned eyes that looked perpetually sad even when she was smirking or smiling, and her head lowered. "I'll be good."

He studied her face a moment. Her thick, wavy black hair pulled back from her face, with a few straggling hairs hanging in her dark eyes. Her chin somewhat pointy, and a spray of freckles across her nose and high cheekbones. He had to admit, she was an attractive woman.

Now's not the time, Mike.

He approached the edge of the bed and leaned over her, close to that pretty face. He uncuffed her left wrist and she looked up at him, fluttering her eye-lashes at him as she slid the cuffs off the headboard and rubbed her wrist.

Enhart stood abruptly, stiffly.

Women had attempted to seduce him many times. Men too, once or twice. He knew, if he hadn't been in the job he was—which put him in a position of power over them, if only temporarily—those same women and men wouldn't have looked at him twice.

He wasn't conventionally attractive, and he knew he'd gotten lucky with Christie-Ann. She'd been sitting across from him at one of those greasy-spoon diners—this one a truck stop in Buckhannon, West Virginia—coincidentally reading John Steinbeck's *Of Mice and Men*, his favorite book since he was a kid. He'd struck up a conversation with her about it, then she'd sat down at his table, and by the time the waitress came around to freshen up their coffees they'd fallen into an easy conversation about anything and everything and forgotten all about the book.

Aside from her slightly aggravating fad diets and his job, he and Christie-Ann had just about everything else in common.

"You didn't bring my chair, did you?"

He shrugged, swallowing hard. "Sorry."

Gloria sighed herself. "Well, I guess you're gonna have to carry me."

"Guess so."

Awkwardly, because of the handcuffs hanging from her right wrist, she lifted her legs one at a time, moving them so her calves flopped off the edge of the bed. Then she turned her upper body to face him. Stupidly, he'd put her in the middle of the bed, hadn't even considered seating her closer to the edge. Fortunately, it was only a double.

"You're gonna have to lift me from here, champ."

With an "Oopsie-daisy," Enhart scooped her up under the arms. She hung limply, her full weight—which wasn't much, to be fair—pressed against his chest.

"Oopsie-daisy?" she said, her chin resting on his shoulder and her breath in his ear. "Really?"

"Yeah, sorry. Been practicing for the baby."

"I bet. Is she...?"

"She was born a few weeks premature. We're just waiting on the doctors to send her—" He shifted her weight slightly. Gloria's legs inadvertently rubbed against his crotch and he shifted her to the side. "Let's get you to the bathroom, huh?"

"Please."

He carried her over. "Should I just sit you on the toilet or...?"

"I can take my pants off by myself, Michael. How do you think I do it at home?"

He shimmied her over to the toilet. Her legs pressed heavily against his groin as he lifted the lid with a foot, then lowered her to the seat.

"Thank you," she said.

"No problem."

Enhart slipped out quickly and closed the door behind him before adjusting the crotch of his pants so his suddenly heavier dick fell to the side. He hadn't had sex with Christie-Ann since she started showing —she was worried about traumatizing the baby, which he thought was complimentary but unwarranted, not to mention frustrating—and the result was him standing at half-mast with a little bit of accidental rubbing from an attractive young woman who —even if he hadn't been happily married—was one-hundred percent off limits.

Not only was it against everything he believed in, it would spoil any chance he had at getting her out of that cult.

This *three miracles* game of hers, he'd gone along with it so she'd open up about the Children of Dinah. The more he could discredit her beliefs, the closer he'd get to winning her over. And the first step was making her talk about the people she lived with, their leader—a woman, apparently, not a man as Bob Ingles and other speculators in their profession had assumed —and their beliefs.

A light tinkle of urine striking the bowl and splashing into the water made him more uncomfortable. "So what happened to Dinah?" he called with his back to the door, hoping to mask the sound of her urinating. "I mean Chloe."

"Well," Gloria said, loud enough to be heard through the door while still peeing, "Chloe's dad dragged the exorcist off of her and beat on him until her mom convinced him to stop." Enhart heard her tear off a scrap of toilet paper as she continued. "After the men got their clothes sorted, the exorcist claimed that when he'd finally been able to cast the demon out of her it must've temporarily entered the two of them, possessing them to perform 'abhorrent acts of carnality.'"

Enhart huffed a laugh. "Sneaky fuck."

She grunted, and the jingle of the cuffs indicating she was pulling up her pants. "Dad didn't buy it," she said, "but after a while Father Epsilon and the exorcist managed to calm him down and eventually swayed him toward their version of things. I'm done."

"You're done?"

"You can come in now," she said, slightly annoyed.

Enhart opened the door. She was sitting on the seat with her pants pulled up.

"I can't reach the sink."

She held up her arms. He bent to pick her up, then realized he'd have to turn around so she could wash her hands.

"I'm gonna have to pick you up from behind. Is that okay?"

"Interesting that *now* consent is important to you."

"Funny."

She rolled her eyes. "Yes, you can pick me up from behind."

Enhart crouched dutifully, reaching in between her and the toilet tank to scoop her up into his arms again. Her ass slumped against his already tumescent bulge and moved back and forth with each pump of his legs as he shimmied her over to the sink.

"This would've been a lot easier if you'd brought my chair."

"Tell me about it."

As she reached over the sink and ran the taps, Enhart thought about his little baby girl in the incubator at the hospital. He thought about how frightening it'd been when Christie-Ann had to deliver her eight weeks early. She was such a tiny, fragile thing, red-hued and seemingly angry to have been yanked too soon from her cozy home inside of her mother.

Gloria washed and dried her hands, and Enhart managed to stave off an erection.

"I forgot to flush," she said, as he turned to leave.

"I'll get it later." He carried her back to the bed. "Now what?" he said, realizing she was facing the wrong way.

"Just lay me down on the bed and I'll get myself turned around."

He lowered her onto the bed. He watched a moment as she rolled onto her back, her breasts jostling under the loose hemp top, then looked away until she was seated.

Good God, it's like you've never seen a pretty girl before. How many times have you been in this same exact position? Thirty? Forty? Get it together, Mike.

Finally, she managed to pull herself up with the headboard to a seated position, and yanked down her shirt that had pulled up, revealing multiple puckered scars on her midriff and ribs. "You know you don't *have* to cuff me. I'm not going anywhere."

"Not without your wheelchair."

"Not in the middle of *The Gospel*," she said pointedly.

Enhart let out a laugh through his nose. He plopped down in the chair opposite the bed—what they'd started calling the 'cuck chair' online, even though it was clearly so guests didn't have to always sit on the bed or at the desk—eager to get off his feet. She was probably a hundred pounds soaking wet but lifting her around had him a bit winded. *It's all that low-protein, high-carb shit Christie-Ann's been feeding me*, he thought. Although it could just as easily be the high-fat, high-calorie diet he'd been on the past couple of days from the Land's End Diner.

"All right, Gloria. No handcuffs, as long as we can trust each other for now."

"Thank you."

"So where were we?"

"The men were arguing downstairs," Gloria continued.

"Right."

"And Mom consoled Chloe in their bedroom, where Chloe told her everything. That Father Epsilon had been touching her in the confession booth and in his office, wherever he could get his disgusting hands on her. He'd even—well, you don't want to hear about that part, but it was the inspiration for those drawings of hers I mentioned. The ones that started all of this talk about demonic possession.

"Once Mom got Chloe to sleep with the help of half of one of her Valiums, she went downstairs and spoke to Dad alone in the kitchen. She didn't believe their version of events, and Dad wasn't buying it either, but they both agreed that Father Epsilon's position was too prominent for the town to withstand the scandal, and since they didn't want to bring what they decided was 'unjust scrutiny' against the Catholic church—seeing as it wasn't the fault of the diocese or the bishop or even God Himself that one of His men of the cloth abused the power vested in him, at least in their opinions—Mom and Dad agreed to sweep it under the rug, so long as Epsilon promised to transfer to another diocese and Petrichor left town and never came back. It was less than what Dad *wanted* to do to the exorcist, but since murder was immoral, not to mention illegal, they let him go with the promise that Dad would 'kill him with his bare hands' if he heard of an exorcism happening within a hundred miles of them."

"They got off easy." Enhart considered adding *so to speak*, but decided it wasn't the time.

"They did," Gloria agreed. "After that night, Chloe was a little more withdrawn than she was before it all started, but her grades and attentiveness went back up. She went back to bathing and brushing her teeth and dressing normally without coercion, started hanging out with a few of her old friends. She even started eating again, more than she used to, actually. Life went back to normal, for a time."

"That's good."

"It was. Until about a month later when she started getting sick, every morning like clockwork."

"Oh no," Enhart said, remembering Christie-Ann's morning routine in the first trimester of her pregnancy.

"You guessed it. Turned out Chloe was pregnant, though they didn't know if it was with the exorcist's demon spawn or Father Epsilon's unholy seed, not that it mattered either way. If Mom or Dad had a sister, they probably would've asked if Chloe could live with them until she had the baby, then make her give the kid up for adoption. But Mom was an only child, and Dad just had an unmarried brother. So they sent her to live at a convent, like some families still did back then, even though it was the Catholic Church that got her into that mess in the first place."

"Oh boy," Enhart said.

"Fortunately for Chloe, most of the nuns were fine. A few were stricter than others, but it was better than the treatment she'd gotten from Father Epsilon. Life was fine there, though she missed her parents and her friends and even school, a little. And life at the convent continued to be fine until her twenty-sixth week, when a placental abruption caused her to give birth early.

"After she recovered a few weeks later, and the baby was adopted, the nuns sent her home. She returned to school, and things immediately went back to normal. Strangely so, her parents thought. By the time she graduated from high school, it seemed like she'd forgotten all about her trauma and her baby, and obviously her parents were never going to bring it up. It was almost like none of it'd ever happened, despite what they'd seen that night etched indelibly into their minds.

"Weirder still, Chloe decided to join a convent instead of college or the 'gap year' some of her friends were taking. Despite all that'd happened to her, she'd never stopped praying every night before bed or saying grace before supper. In fact, she *prayed more*, especially after she came back from the convent. And it wasn't like she'd had any boyfriends since. They didn't expect her to get married, and they were relatively certain she wasn't eager to get pregnant again either.

"So, it was the cloistered life for Chloe, at the same convent, although this time around they called her *Sister Amelia*, going by her middle name. Just like in school, Chloe—now Sister Amelia—excelled in the choir. Visits with her parents were few and far between. It was better for them, if they were being honest with themselves, because every time they saw her they remembered the way they'd seen her that night, with Father Epsilon and the exorcist doing what they'd done to her.

"Three years later, after she took her vows, she was assigned to a church very far from home. The priest there had asked for her specifically, because as he said, her voice was 'like that of the angels themselves.' Sister Amelia's Mother Superior thought his words were somewhat blasphemous, but agreed that God did give the young woman a lovely singing voice. If Father Epsilon wanted her to lead his choir, it was fine by her."

"Here we go" Enhart said.

"A week later, Sister Amelia and Father Epsilon stood face to face in his office. He shook her hand, he

45

smiled and told her how lovely he thought her voice was, and he didn't seem to recognize her at all. She'd grown into a beautiful young woman since they'd last seen each other. Father Epsilon, on the other hands, looked much older, almost decrepit, as if time had taken out her revenge on his body."

"Good."

"Chloe thought so too. But not good enough. She hadn't turned the other cheek, although you probably already guessed that. She'd been searching for him, actually. Him and the exorcist. Calling around from one diocese to the next from the payphone in a bad neighborhood a few blocks from the convent. The fact that Father Epsilon himself had sought her out for his choir was providence. She would be the hand of God's Wrath. She'd be Divine Justice."

"I don't believe in revenge," Enhart said, "Was it Ghandi who said 'an eye for an eye leaves the whole world blind'?"

Gloria shrugged. "Sounds like something he'd say," she said dismissively.

"I understand the feeling, don't get me wrong. Something like that, it'd be hard to bounce back from. If someone hurt my kid in that way—" He stopped abruptly.

She seemed to soften then. "What's her name?"

"We haven't decided yet," he lied.

Gloria eyed him for a long moment in obvious disbelief before continuing.

SISTER AMELIA WAITED months to take her revenge on Father Epsilon. And while she waited, she tested him. Making subtle sexual innuendos, gestures, expressions. Flirting without being overt about it, lest the deacon and others realize it. She was trying to see if he'd slip up, if he'd fall into her trap, or if he'd truly been repentant. Not that it mattered to her if he was. In fact, it would be *better* if he thought God had forgiven him. And it seemed that Epsilon was penitent. He did everything by the book while Sister Amelia worked in his parish. It really seemed like he'd cleaned up his act. But Sister Amelia knew what he was capable of, and she watched him from the shadows, particularly the times he was with the children. But she noticed, he'd never positioned himself so he'd be alone with any single child, not like when she was little. If a young boy or girl required guidance, he'd ask Sister Amelia or a deacon to step in with prayers, confessions and other spiritual matters.

It was almost like Epsilon was doing everything he could to avoid temptation. She was glad for it, even if a part of her envied those children their innocence. But it meant the temptation was still in him. He still *wanted* to abuse them. He was just fighting the urge. Struggling with that demon.

All the while, Sister Amelia used the church's resources to track down the exorcist. She remembered his name—she'd been listening in on the night he introduced himself to her parents—and since he wasn't an ordained priest, it was likely any exorcism he performed wasn't sanctioned by the Catholic Church. They might end up in the news or church correspondence, or the priest himself might've still been in contact with him. After no luck for months—years really, if you counted the time she'd spent rooting through Mother Superior's office at the convent while the other women slept—she finally found mention of Petrichor in an article in a men's magazine. With the *Exorcist* movie out a couple of years prior, exorcisms were back in style, and Paul Petrichor had found himself a little bit of fame. His interview quotes showed him as arrogant as ever, and Sister Amelia grew even more eager to take him down.

He was working out of Cincinnati, and she found his address from an ad in the Cincinnatti phone book. She wrote to him, copying Father Epsilon's handwriting as well as she could, telling him the police were asking questions about young girls in his old parish, and they'd need to meet urgently at his church to decide how to proceed or the two of them would be ruined. Or *worse*. Excommunicated. Thrown in prison.

She wrote as if Father Epsilon had been pushed to the edge, because she wanted Petrichor scared. A cornered rat will lunge and bite, and that was exactly what she wanted from him.

When she finished, she faxed the letter to Petrichor's office. She didn't expect to get an answer right away, but she did. *Don't say anything*, it said. *Don't do anything. When can we meet?*

The night they agreed on, Sister Amelia sent the other sisters and the deacon out to a movie, and she finally got Father Epsilon all alone in the rectory. Earlier she'd thought he wasn't taking her subtle advances because he wasn't interested in sex anymore, but that wasn't it at all. He wasn't interested in her because she was *too old* for him. But when she showed him a photo of herself as a child, little Chloe Amelia, Father Epsilon's eyes bugged out in his head.

Sister Amelia told him not to worry. She said she'd *liked* what he and the exorcist had done to her. She told him she wanted to do it for him again.

"I mustn't," the priest said, but he licked his lips and squirmed in his chair. He was staring at the photo she'd laid in front of him, of her at twelve years old, barely a year before her confirmation, the year she'd been possessed by two grown men.

"But I *must*," she said, and she lifted up the hem of her habit, giving him an eyeful of the white pantyhose she'd bought specifically for this encounter, just like the nuns in the confiscated men's magazines she'd found in Mother Superior's desk. The priest's eyes darted to her thighs momentarily, then returned to the old photograph. Reading his mind, she grinned slyly and crawled under his desk.

Crouching between his legs, she found him already stiff as a crucifix. He let out a troubled moan as she unzipped his pants and pulled the fleshy scepter out of his underpants. He looked different down there than she remembered. Sagging, wrinkled flesh speckled with liver spots, his salt-and-pepper pubic hair coiled like the scouring pads she used on the old cooking pots in the church kitchen.

She gripped Father Epsilon around the shaft, tugging gently on his foreskin. His whole body shuddered with illicit pleasure. Looking up she could see he was already getting too excited, so she slowed down. Because she didn't want him to cum, and she wanted him just hard enough he'd be too consumed with pleasure to understand what was happening to him until it was already too late.

"Keep going," the priest moaned.

She didn't need his permission, but she appreciated the enthusiasm. Because this next part would be less than pleasant for him. She slipped the surgical scissors out from the hem of her pantyhose and eased them toward Epsilon's semihard penis, glancing up to see if he was watching her. But his eyes were set on her twelve-year-old self, the little girl she'd abandoned in her quest for revenge.

Fingers trembling, she pulled his foreskin over the tip of his penis and inserted the blade. She looked up again, but the priest was fully focused on the object of his lust.

So she snipped, making the "dorsal slit" she'd read about in the medical texts in Mother Superior's office.

The priest roared in pain, but as his blood poured out of him so did his cum, spurting out spasmodically as she gripped him in place by the cock and balls, mingling with the blood.

"*FUCKING HELL,*" Enhart hissed, crossing his legs with a wince. Cutting the priest's foreskin was bad enough, but the description of him ejaculating while bleeding from the tip was just too much. Especially since the part about the nun jerking off the priest had started to turn Enhart on again, as Gloria had mimed the action, pumping a fist slowly as she'd said it while—seemingly deliberately—holding his gaze.

Control yourself, Mike, he warned himself.

Gloria grinned at him. "You're gonna have a difficult time with these stories if you can't take a little blood," she said.

"Sorry." He shrugged. "I'll try to limit my interruptions."

"If you don't mind."

"Sure. Keep going," he said, realizing too late it was exactly what the priest had just said to Sister Amelia.

At least I didn't moan it, he thought bitterly.

"IF YOU MOVE," Sister Amelia warned the priest, "I'll cut off the whole package. I'm just taking the fore-skin," she said. "Dinah's revenge on the men of Shechem. Remember them?"

Father Epsilon howled in pain.

Sister Amelia gripped him harder, his wrinkled balls shiny and taut like the end of a squeezed balloon, her hand covered in glistening crimson. "Nod if you remember," she said forcefully.

The priest nodded.

"This is going to hurt, Father," she told him. "But not as badly as you hurt me. Keep looking at that little girl. Do you see her? I want you to *feel* how much you hurt her. You understand?"

Tears spilled down the old man's cheeks.

"Tell me you understand!" she yelled at him, still crouched between his legs.

"I-I-I—"

She moved the tips of the shears to where she held his ballooned ballsack in a death grip, and the priest nodded fiercely, tears flying from his cheeks.

"I understand!" he yelped.

Sister Amelia let go of his balls, back to gripping the shaft of his withered penis. "This is gonna hurt like Hell," she said, then snipped.

The priest wailed in unholy agony.

"Keep looking at her, Father! Remember Chloe! Remember Dinah!"

She chanted this as she snipped the foreskin away from the head of his penis—*snip! snip! snip!*—the priest punctuating every slice of his flesh with an ago-nized howl that reminded her of his sighs and moans during their last exorcism. Thinking this made each successive snip even more of a delight for her.

"This is an *exorcism*, Father!" she shouted up at him with sadistic glee. "We'll cut the Devil out of you yet!"

One final snip and the flap of severed flesh fell to the floor with a small wet splat. Sister Amelia let go of the priest's shaft, satisfied with the job she'd done. Father Epsilon slumped against the back of his leather chair, gripping his mangled penis to stop the flow of blood.

Sister Amelia rose from under the desk and stood over him with a gleeful smile, the perfect personification of God's Wrath. She reached into the large front pocket of her habit and threw a towel at him.

Epsilon took the towel and held it over his groin.

"Do you feel better now, Father?" she asked him. "Do you feel like God's forgiven you?"

The priest looked up at her with sad, tired eyes, and the little boy pout he gave her as he nodded almost convinced her not to keep going. But Dinah's revenge wasn't just circumcision. Her brothers had slaughtered the men of Shechem, every last one of them. They'd kidnapped their wives and mothers and children and took everything of value from their homes.

Besides, the other man of Shechem hadn't arrived yet.

Paul Petrichor arrived twenty minutes early. Sister Amelia had planned to be out of Epsilon's office by the time he arrived, and to try and trick him into shooting the priest, but she wasn't ready. She still had blood on her hands. So she slapped a piece of tape over Father Epsilon's mouth, then turned out the overhead lights and flicked on a light behind him like the villain from some movie she could barely remember watching. Then she crouched behind his chair and waited, as the exorcist called out to Father Epsilon.

"Amos! Amos, you bastard, where are you?"

Amos was sitting behind his desk, slowly bleeding to death from his mutilated penis.

Sister Amelia whispered into his ear, "If you make a sound, I'll kill you." She pressed the scissors against his jugular to make her point.

Barely a second later, the office door burst open. Petrichor stood in silhouette in the doorway, the gun she'd hoped he would bring gripped in his right hand, the same hand that'd done such awful things to her when she was still too young to process them.

But she'd had plenty of time to process them in the years since, working mostly in silence in the convent and the church. When her parents surprised them that night, she'd seen fear, *actual unholy terror*, in the eyes of Paul Petrichor and Father Epsilon for the first time. Their sadistic masks of authority had slipped for those few perfect minutes as her dad beat the exorcist to a pulp, and young Chloe Amelia had felt a glimmer of hope for the first time since the priest had abused her at the age of nine, when she'd started developing breasts.

God had shown her, while the priest dressed himself and Dad pummeled the exorcist, that *power is malleable*.

The priest had power over her because she'd been just a little girl, and no one would believe one little girl over the man who'd been their spiritual leader for thirty-five years.

Her parents had power over the priest and the exorcist because what they'd seen had not just been wrong but *illegal*, and because Dad was stronger than Paul Petrichor.

Now, Sister Amelia was the one with the power. She had power over the priest because of her sexuality, and his weakness of the flesh. And she had power over Petrichor because of his quickness to anger, his fragile ego, and his fear of getting caught.

"I'm going to confess, Paul," she said, deepening her voice to sound like Father Epsilon, though she didn't really sound much like him at all. She just had to hope that the exorcist's fear outweighed his senses. "There's nothing you can do to stop me."

Father Epsilon shook his head, but he stopped when Sister Amelia pressed the scissors deeper into his flesh, drawing a bead of blood from his withered flesh.

"We had some good times together, Padre," the exorcist said, raising the gun. "I really am sorry about this."

Father Epsilon moaned under the tape. Sister Amelia made to stab him, but the exorcist fired and she ducked as Father Epsilon's body jumped in the chair with each bullet striking him, once, twice, three times. As she crouched, waiting for the right opportunity, the priest's right hand, the hand that had stolen her innocence all those years ago, slipped off the armrest and dripped blood onto her cheek.

In the following silence, she stood up abruptly, twisting the lamp to shine it directly in Petrichor's face. He raised a hand to shield his eyes and she ran at him across the room. The exorcist fired blindly. One shot hit the books on the shelf behind her just after she passed them, another struck Father Epsilon's Master of Theology degree off the wall. It shattered on the floor at her feet and she kept running, over the shards of glass.

The third and hopefully final bullet—it was a revolver, and he'd already shot the priest three times—

struck her in the shoulder and spun her halfway around, but she didn't let it stop her. She *couldn't*.

She was Vengeance. She was God's Holy Wrath.

The nun, the victim, the avenger, she rushed her abuser, stabbing him multiple times in the chest and stomach in rapid succession like a prisoner with a shank.

Petrichor dropped the gun and grabbed her by the throat, squeezing the life out of her, but the more she stabbed him, the more his grip weakened. She must've stabbed him twenty times when he let her go finally and fell to the floor, his gritted teeth stained pink with blood. She fell against him with the scissors poised over his beard-stubbled jugular, ready to snip.

Like Father Epsilon, he looked like he'd aged several decades in the time since the last exorcism. His nose looked like an overripe strawberry and his eyes were bloodshot and bleary. That along with his whiskey breath were classic signs of chronic alcoholism. The thought of his life falling to pieces because of what they'd done to her made her smile, the first genuine smile she could remember since they took her childhood away from her.

"Please," the exorcist gasped. His lungs whistled through a sucking wound in his chest. "*Please...*"

"I said *please* too, remember?"

The pathetic, dying man's eyes widened, staring up at her. "You were just... a stupid kid," he said between ragged breaths.

"I'm not a kid anymore," she told him, and she jabbed the scissors into his neck. A hot geyser of blood splashed over her. She stood and looked down at him as the life left his eyes and the blood spurted weaker and weaker, until it was just a dribble, and he expelled his final breath.

It was over.

The exorcist's death hadn't played out like she'd expected. She'd hoped, after he shot Father Epsilon, to seduce the exorcist the way she had the priest, then brutally circumcise him before cutting his life short, like Dinah's brothers had to the men of Shechem.

It hadn't happened that way, and she'd been injured in the process. She was bleeding badly. The exorcist had shot her in the shoulder. She had to remove the bullet and sew herself up with the medical kit. Still, she was grateful God had given her the opportunity for revenge.

So that's what Mother Amelia shares with us: Her children. We're all Children of Dinah, Mother Amelia included, and we've all been given the chance to be born again through Her Light and Wisdom. Vengeance sets us free from our pasts, Michael. From the transgressions imposed upon us by evil men and women.

"Bullshit," Enhart said.

Gloria smirked. "You don't believe Her story?"

"No. What you said about vengeance. I don't believe the act of killing another person ever solves anything."

"What about capital punishment?"

"Nope. Even with DNA evidence, they still get it wrong. You're telling me you trust your neighbors enough to decide whether or not you should go to the electric chair?"

"So you're a pacifist. Like Ghandi."

Enhart shrugged. "I'm not a pacifist, no. If

someone hits me, I'm not turning the other cheek so they can hit me again. But I don't believe in murder."

"What about war?"

"That's different."

"How?"

"War is..." He thought a moment. "It's a last resort against international aggression. A greater good situation."

"Not always."

"Sure. There are other reasons for war. Ulterior motives and whatnot. But war is often necessary to prevent further atrocities. World War II, for instance."

"We're getting off topic. We're talking about revenge. You don't believe revenge can be healing."

"No," he said decisively. "I don't."

Gloria sat up, studying his face, his hands. "Did someone abuse you, Michael? When you were young, did someone hurt you?"

Enhart flinched. "No," he said, shaking his head a little too strongly. "Nobody ever... nobody *touched* me... like that. And even if they did, it's no excuse for me to *kill* them. I don't know if I could forgive something like that. Not exactly. It'd be hard. But forgiveness has to be healthier than murder. Forgiveness. Love. That's harder for people to do than hate. That's what makes it *stronger*. Makes *us* stronger. Whether or not you think of Jesus as a hypocrite, that's what He taught. Love and forgiveness of your fellow man."

"And woman," Gloria said, holding his gaze.

He crossed his arms and stared back, like the man gazing into Nietzsche's abyss.

"I don't think you believe all that, Michael. You *say* it, and I feel like you've said it a hundred times before. But it sounds like a kid reciting the Pledge of Allegiance, like a C and E Catholic reciting the Lord's

Prayer, or a roomful of drunks chanting the Serenity Prayer when they know in their hearts they're just one disaster away from falling off the wagon. Everything about you—your body language, your expression, your eyes—they're *screaming* a very different story."

"Speaking of," he said, eager to change the subject. "You still haven't told me about those 'three miracles' of yours."

Gloria blinked at him. Then she nodded. "We'll circle back to this," she said. "Let's talk about miracles then."

Enhart's cell phone rang. He thought he'd put it on vibrate, was sure of it, but still the ringtone blared from the inner pocket of his jacket, hung from one of the coat hooks by the door. He sighed and crossed to it, tugged it out and frowned as he looked at the screen. The ringtone—one of the standard jingles that came with the phone, nothing fancy or personal—continued blaring.

"I have to take this," he said.

Gloria sat up straighter with a look of innocent curiosity.

Enhart turned, unlatched and unlocked the door, then stepped briskly out of the room, shutting the door behind him.

"Hi, honey. What is it? Is the baby okay?"

Christie-Ann spoke. Her anxiety sharp as broken glass.

"Oh, God. Well, what did the doctor say? What are they gonna do about it?" He listened, his own panic rising. "*Surgery?* Jesus!" He waited for her to finish speaking. She was crying now, probably had been before the call and composed herself as well as she could. Christie-Ann had that way about her, able to switch from one emotion to the other seemingly at will. "Well, what do you think? Yes, of course, they should do it if they have to, I'm just... Okay. I said *okay*. Yeah. Let me know the second you hear. Yeah, I love you too, Bunches. Stay strong."

He hung up the phone, his whole world turned upside-down in an instant. He felt numb. His hand trembled as he returned the phone to his pocket, keeping the ringer on.

The baby's appendix had ruptured.

HOLEY

"You know," Enhart said, returning from the bathroom, where he'd splashed cool water on his face while the flush of the toilet masked the sound of running water, "there's this woman who was raped by her high school boyfriend. Years later, she decided to fly halfway across the world to meet up with him and try to forgive him, to put that chapter of her life behind her. Give herself peace. After their meeting, the two of them wrote a book about it. They did a TED Talk and even do speaking tours together."

"How magnanimous of her."

"I'm just saying, revenge isn't the only answer. It *shouldn't be* the only answer. There's a charity that gives victims of all sorts of trauma alternatives to the stuff Mother Amelia taught you. It's called The Forgiveness Project. There's some truly inspiring stories—"

"Who was that on the phone, Michael?" Gloria interrupted. "You looked like somebody told you your mother just died when you came back in."

Enhart huffed. If only it were that. But he hadn't looked like someone had told him his mother died when he'd splashed cold water on his face. He knew exactly what he looked like when that happened, and it wasn't the same. This was shock. When he'd learned of his mother's death, the year he'd turned thirteen, he'd skipped over that stage of grief entirely and gone straight to anger. At his father, at his mom, at himself.

He knew exactly what that expression looked like because he'd lived with it for years, until he'd finally decided to stop wasting anger and heartache over a woman who'd been gone for decades.

"No," he said. "My mother died a long time ago, Gloria. Let's talk about your mother."

"Not this again."

"Mother Amelia, I mean. You told me how she supposedly freed herself from *her* traumas. Tell me more about what *she* does for *you*. How she helps you people recover from the traumas holding *you* back from self-actualization."

Gloria nodded thoughtfully. "All right. You want to hear my story, do you?"

"That's what we're here for, Gloria. This is all about you."

She smirked.

"What?" he asked.

"It's just funny you said that. I was thinking the same about you."

He frowned. "What's that supposed to mean?"

She let it hang a moment. Then she said, "I don't think you do this for the money. And definitely not about altruism."

"Why do you think I do it then?" he asked, a little too defensively, barely managing to stop himself from crossing his arms again.

Gloria studied his face a moment longer. "I'm not sure yet. But okay, I'll tell you my story, Michael. Because *that's what we're here for*," she said pointedly, and Enhart huffed. "It all started when I was seventeen. My friends and me got in a car accident on our way to prom. My boyfriend was driving. My best friend Pearl and I were in the backseat, and her boyfriend Davis was riding shotgun. We'd had a few drinks at Pearl's house. Her parents were away a lot and they had a liquor cabinet and never noticed we'd been adding pop to the bottles because they never drank any of it. You know, typical kids having a good time. Jackson, my boyfriend, he'd only had one beer. He was nursing it all night because he knew he'd be driving, and he was good like that. He didn't need alcohol to have a good time. He didn't need it to *be* a good time. Just a naturally fun, caring person who made everyone feel like they were the center of attention. For a high school senior, center field on the baseball team, good grades, he really was one of a kind.

"The other driver was a trucker who'd been on the road for eighteen hours straight. They said he fell asleep at the wheel and veered off onto our side of the road, while we were on a bend. Jackson got crushed when the steering wheel and dashboard crumpled into his body. His lungs collapsed and he died within a few minutes. Davis, who drank more than any of us that night, his body went slack against the airbag and he was barely injured aside from a broken nose. Pearl had been bending over to get her phone that'd fallen between her feet while she was trying to show me pictures of her and Davis's camping trip the weekend before. Her head hit the back of Davis's seat and she suffered a cervical fracture roughly similar to someone executed by hanging. She died almost instantly.

"As for me, I was thrown forward so violently that the lap belt fractured my spine at the L2 vertebrae, completely paralyzing me from the waist down. I *saw* my legs were twisted and broken from the frame of the driver's seat slamming into them, and the lower half of my baby blue prom dress was drenched in blood like Carrie White, but I couldn't *feel* anything. The EMTs said I was lucky. They said the pain would've been bad enough to pass out. If that'd happened, I would've died in the fire with the rest of them."

Enhart shuddered. The phrasing was almost too perfect. *'Died in the fire with the rest of them,'* he thought. *That could've been me.* "Your mother," he said, desperate to stay on track, "she emailed me the X-rays. Those were some nasty breaks."

Gloria nodded somberly. "I was just able to unlock my door and spill out onto the road. Scraped up my hands real bad—that I *could* feel. My legs weren't working, but I thought it was because they were broken. I could see the bone sticking out of my left shin. I was barely able to pull myself to the side of the road before the car caught fire.

"You say 'small miracles'? Was it a miracle that I survived? Maybe. A miracle's an act of God, of divine intervention. So was it a miracle when I had to lie on the side of the road waiting for someone to help us, smelling my best friend's and my boyfriend's bodies *cooking* in that fire, having to listen to the only other person who survived *scream for minutes* as he burned alive, pinned in his seat? Was *that* a miracle, Michael? Was *that* divine intervention? Or was the miracle, that little twist of fate, was it the truck driver veering off onto our side of the road, and me pulling myself from the wreck and surviving the crash just dumb luck?"

"What do you mean by that?"

"I mean, why do we consider it a miracle, an act of

God, of *divine intervention*," she said, pointing up accusatorily at the ceiling, "when those little quirks of fate just so happen to fall in our favor? How can we say for certain God's not up there watching all of us, all the time, toying with us like a sadistic little kid burning ants under a magnifying glass?"

Enhart shook his head. "Are you asking me that?"

"Yes. I'm asking you why one thing is considered a miracle and the other is just an awful thing that happened."

He thought of Christie-Ann's phone call. Jessa's appendix rupturing—perforated appendicitis, she'd said—was just about the most awful thing he could imagine. Jessa could die in that surgery, but she'd die if they didn't perform it. If Enhart hadn't kidnapped Gloria just three hours prior, if he wasn't holding her here against her will, he'd have driven straight to the hospital to be by their side. Most of the past two weeks since Christie-Ann had the C-section he'd spent doing his research on the Children of Dinah and recon at the compound. As much as he wanted to be there with them every minute of the day, he still had to pay the bills.

What were the odds Jessa's appendix would burst now, of all times?

"I don't know," he answered her. "Free will? The way I figure, if you believe in God, or the Judeo-Christian God specifically, it's like we're tops He sets to spinning on the day we're born. We bump into each other, we stumble and fall, but the outcome of our lives isn't preordained, because He gave us free will. Outside of acts of nature, things happen in life because of our decisions, our natures, our interactions with each other. But miracles? I already told you, I don't believe in em."

"Well, I *do* believe in miracles," Gloria said. "Because I've experienced them firsthand."

"So you've said. But it doesn't sound like you think surviving that accident was a miracle."

"No. I didn't believe in God back then. And after that night, I decided any god who'd spare my life just so I could live through what came next wasn't someone I wanted to spend any of my time worshipping."

"Your mother—*the woman who raised you*," he corrected himself swiftly, "said your recovery was rough."

"It was. Even worse, I never got to model again. I used to get a lot of gigs too. But then there was the recovery, and the scars on my legs and the small of my back...." Gloria pulled up the bottoms of her hemp pajamas, revealing several pale scars up her shins on both of her otherwise tanned legs. "Nobody wanted a paraplegic model. Even now, things have gotten better, more progressive, but when's the last time you saw a runway model in a chair, or using crutches. And there's only so many poses you can do lying down. I sure as hell wasn't interested in posing for the kind of magazines with more than a handful. No pun intended."

Enhart chuckled.

"So I quit modeling, or modeling quit me, I guess is more accurate. Like Chloe, my grades took a beating when I finally went back to school, and it was tough, going back there. After all the operations and recovery, I was almost a year behind, and... to be honest, I felt like nobody wanted to look at me. Not only did looking at me remind them three of the most popular kids in school died in a flaming car crash, but here I was rolling around the halls in a wheelchair. On a good day, most people ignored me if I wasn't trying to open a door or something else where they'd have to feel obligated to help me. Even some of the teachers talked to me like my accident, what I'd started to refer to as my 'Little Act of God,' left me deaf or mentally challenged."

Enhart shook his head. "A lot of people don't know how to handle disabilities."

"Right. And some of the worst are the ones who say things like, 'she's not disabled, she's just *differently abled*.' Patronizing bullshit. Okay, there's some things I can do better than other people 'cause of what I had to learn to cope with my disability, but I know my limitations. Just because I live with it, doesn't mean I have to *embrace* it."

"Got it. No 'differently abled' for you."

"Fuck no. Fuck 'handi-capable' all the way to the moon and back too. And I don't believe for a minute these people that act like they wouldn't trade just about *anything* to get out of their chair. To walk along the water's edge and feel the sand between your toes. To dance." He saw that sparkle in her eyes again, as he had when they'd first spoken about Dinah's revenge. Then it faded. "Like the chair defines them as a person," she finished.

He nodded thoughtfully. "So then what happened?"

"I graduated high school, just barely. Didn't even think about going to senior prom. After that, I became sort of lost. I'd always planned to go to drama school after I graduated but that didn't seem attainable anymore, even though my parents still kept pushing me to try. I spent an aimless summer lying by the pool, reading trashy romance novels. You know the ones: the naïve female main character with financial struggles meets the bad boy billionaire."

"Like uh... that *Fifteen Shades* one."

"Fifty *Shades*," she corrected him with a slight grin. "That one got pretty big the summer after my accident. So that's what I did that summer by the pool. I didn't even get in the water. I guess I was afraid I might drown, even with all the physio I had to do during recovery, since my parents were at work most days. My arms were pretty strong from the chair, I know I *could've* swam without the use of my legs, but... I still wasn't strong enough *mentally*. So I lay there on the lounger, day after day, reading about not-so-strong independent women falling for rich men who ended up being bad for them and seemed to spend too much time working out for them to be very good businessmen, either."

"Sounds like a blast."

Gloria shrugged. "It was fine. But yeah, I was lost." She frowned, glancing up at the painting, though he knew she couldn't see much of it from where she sat. "I think we're all born with a hole in ourselves," she said finally. "As we grow, as we become who we're meant to be, we fill that hole with love, with family, with purpose—"

"With God?" Enhart suggested, inadvertently glancing at the father and son in the painting.

"Some of us," Gloria agreed. "For others, a literal god might not be the answer. Some people find God in the bottom of a bottle, or in a needle, or between someone's legs, or lots of someones. For me, before my Little Act of God, it was always modeling and acting. And I still wanted to do those things afterwards. They made some accommodations so I could be in the senior play. But I just couldn't bring myself to take the leap. It was just like the pool. How do you jump in when you can't swim? How do you take that first step when you can't walk?"

Enhart hummed thoughtfully.

"My breakthrough came near the end of summer, when one of my old modeling friends—you don't really have *friends* in modeling, more like frenemies, but that's what we called each other—she called me out of the blue one Friday. She had a big gig at some party in a mansion in the Hollywood Hills, and one of the models had to bail at the last minute. Could I fill in? This girl was a couple years older than me, she had no idea about what happened."

"Oh."

"Yeah. I'd be lying by the pool, and all summer long I was thinking about, 'What if I just dive in?' I could drown, sure. But what if I figure out I can actually swim? Wouldn't it be worth it to try? But I was still too chicken. All summer, too scared to try."

"So what'd you say to her?"

"I asked her what the gig was. She told me, it was super easy. The easiest gig she'd ever taken. The pay was good and the tips could be pretty decent. I'd never gotten tips before so I was suspicious. I asked her, 'It's not like a sex thing, is it?' And she said, no. It's this thing called *nyotaimori*, a Japanese thing that means *body sushi*."

"Like cannibalism?"

Gloria laughed. "Not like cannibalism. Basically, models lie naked on a table, or wearing a G-string and pasties and banana hammocks for men, which was what they asked for at this party. Technically *nyotaimori* means 'serve on the female body,' but Hannah's boss also hired men, which is called *nantaimori*.

And the guests eat sushi and sashimi directly off their bodies."

Enhart grimaced. "Sounds unhygienic."

"For the models or the guests?"

He shrugged. "Both, I guess. I dunno if I'd want raw fish all over my body. Or to eat it off some stranger, not that I like sushi anyway."

"Well, the company has strict washing guidelines. Hot showers with specific soaps before and after gigs. And oh my God, I *love* sushi." She smacked her lips, emphasizing it.

Enhart hummed again. "So I guess you said yes."

"Not right away. There was still the elephant in the room. I knew I'd be fine lying on the table, and I'd had worse gigs, even at seventeen, but I thought, 'Who'd wanna eat off a body with legs covered in scars?' So I told her to give me an hour, I needed to see if I could push a prior engagement. I didn't have anything going on that night, or *any* night. I just needed..." She shrugged a shoulder, the arm with the cuff still hanging from her wrist. "I needed to decide if I could handle the rejection when her boss saw my chair and my scars," she said.

THE FIRST THING I DID, I got back in my chair and rolled to the edge of the pool. I kept looking down at that water between my legs, willing myself to just do it. I knew if I could finally push myself to get in, that would be the first step. That was *taking the plunge*. Literally. If I could do that, I'd be able to take the risk that night. All I had to do was climb down off my chair and sit with my legs over the edge and just... slip in. But the hour was dwindling, and I still couldn't bring myself to do it.

Until finally, it was too late. My phone started ringing and I let out a pathetic, defeated sigh, and I rolled back to the lounger to answer it. Maybe I couldn't get in the water, but this was a *cash job*. Five hundred bucks. I wasn't gonna pass that up just because I couldn't do something that could potentially kill me. I told her I'd be there at the time she said, and I didn't tell her about either the chair or my scars. I just hoped her boss would be too in a jam by the time I got there to care. And I was already used to feeling insecure about my body. The model's curse. Female models, anyway. *Especially* in L.A.

My parents were giddy, especially Tracy. She practically jumped up and down with joy. Sure, they thought it was a strange gig, but they were pretty progressive. I feel like they were probably just glad to see me stop moping around the house.

It's probably weird to you, hearing I had supportive parents but still ended up in what you consider a cult. Most people you talk to come from broken homes, I bet. Abusive parents or siblings. Foster homes. Not me. My family life was good. Just about as close to perfect as you can get.

My dad drove me to the house. We figured the people must be rich. Who else but the rich would spend that kind of money for their friends to eat food off of someone else's body? Plus, they were living in the Bird Streets in the Hollywood Hills. But none of us figured them for *this* rich. The place looked like the White House, only like it was on an old plantation, with all kinds of greenery and big weeping willows and all that. Stuff that'd cost a fortune to grow and mow and keep looking the way it looked. The last listing price when Bill, my dad, looked it up later, was over seventy-six million dollars.

Whoever these people were, whatever they did when they weren't hosting parties where half-naked people acted as serving trays, they were *loaded*.

Hannah's boss walked right up to the car door to greet us, she was that eager to get me started. I opened the door and my dad went around to the back to get my chair. I could see her flinch when he pulled it open, visibly trying not to cringe as he rolled it over to me. When I got out and sat, when she saw my legs, her eyes just about popped out of her head.

Then she quickly composed herself. Beggers can't be choosers. She needed one more woman for the gig and even though she'd been a model herself in her day, her day had long passed. She'd been a high fashion model in the '80s and '90s, and you could tell she wasn't eager to demean herself with a job like this.

So she helped me up to the house, which fortunately had a nice ramp and was otherwise accessible, due to the previous owners being elderly. While she rolled me back to the old servant's quarters, she told me a little about the house and her client, a man named Nathan Rowan. The bad-boy *billionaire* Nathan Rowan, CEO of Rowan Enterprises, a Fortune 500 company founded by his father, Barnard.

Don't worry, this isn't one of my billionaire romance novels. But I did start to wonder what it would've been like if I never had my Little Act of God. If I'd sashayed my pretty little ass into that house like a boss bitch, instead of getting pushed in with my fucked-up legs and my fucked-up back. How many heads I could've turned.

I was egotistical back then, I'll admit it. Before my Little Act of God, it's fair to say I based a lot of my

71

self-worth on my looks. Bill and Tracy supported that. They made sure I had good grades, which always came pretty easy for me, but they put a lot of emphasis on how I looked. Especially Tracy. She had me in beauty pageants by the time I could walk, and I always got the feeling she wished she could've been a model when she was younger, but she was too big-boned. Like she'd been living vicariously through me.

So the miracle did its work. Served His Divine Purpose, I guess. It *humbled* me, so I could discover my *raison d'être*, my reason for being. So I could fill that hole we're all born with. That's what Mother Amelia says. I *thought* I'd filled mine that night, but it turned out I was wrong.

In the beginning it was just like any other runway gig. Aside from the bathing, which was supervised. Hair, makeup, rushing around 'backstage' before the 'show.' Hannah didn't even flinch when she saw me, by the way. She said she actually knew what happened, that's why she 'thought of me first thing.' She also said she wanted to fuck with her boss—*our* boss, at least for that night—Eloise Delice. I told her how Eloise's eyes popped out when she got a look at my legs and we had a good giggle.

Then we went out to our individual tables, Eloise brought my chair to the back, and one of the florists laid down flower arrangements around me. Then the chefs began laying out the sushi, the fruit, vegetables and banana leaves. It tickled at first. Not on my legs or hips, obviously. On my upper body. The chef I got was a young man, bald head. I remember his face very clearly because he had a long, light scar on his face that made me conscious of my own scars. He was very particular about the placement of the food. Very delicate. He never once looked me in the eye, but it didn't seem like a conscious effort. I was a serving dish to him. An inanimate object.

The sauces, the wasabi and all that, they put them in dishes, not on our bodies. I can't even imagine what wasabi would feel like trying to wash out of your... holes. Not for me, obviously. But the others. I did get some on my nipples, not that night, but another time. That burned enough.

The party was lush. There was a live band, light jazz, and everyone dressed up like at a gala. These people didn't just have money, they had *wealth*. It was interesting. You could tell a lot of them were excited to try it, eating raw fish off of people's bodies. Some were nervous, others were... it's more flesh than a lot of people are used to seeing outside of the beach or Beverly Hills, especially treated the way it is. Then people started crowding around my table. Some of them asked me things, but we aren't supposed to talk too much, and we're not supposed to move, so I figured out real quick how not to laugh with my belly. Obviously not moving the rest of my body wasn't a problem. One or two of the other new people had issues, I heard. Restless legs, and all that.

It's not just the models who've got their dos and don'ts. There are certain rules that apply at pretty much every body sushi event for the guests too. Be respectful. Don't chat up the models. But mostly, don't eat the food directly off of a model's body, and *never* use your fingers. *Chopsticks only*. That's mandatory.

A little while later, after I'd already gotten used to all of the attention—or lack of it, depending on the person, like the chef with the facial scar—a couple of young guys were hanging around me, kind of leering at me, like they were trying to decide if they gave me enough cash I'd do stuff for them in the bathroom or the backseat of their car. One of them eventually made a pass at me—something really stupid, I can't even remember it now. I brushed him off with a playful joke about his masculinity I thought was pretty clever.

The guy's friend laughed. The guy didn't. He said something really snarky like I probably taste like bad sushi. The usual sort of half-witty, dismissive comment guys like that make when their pride's wounded. I was just glad the chef'd come around to cover up my scars with another fresh round of food before those two clowns got to my table. I don't know if I could've handled a comment about my body in that moment.

Then he grabbed a piece of sashimi with his fingers from the leaf just above my G-string.

"Chopsticks only," I reminded him, knowing he already knew the rules and was breaking them deliberately to show he had the power. I found out later he was the nephew of some famous movie producer.

Just then another guy came to the table and told the asshole and his friend to move to another table. My white knight. The asshole goes to leave, then turns back with a "You know what? I'm still hungry," and grabs at me again. I dunno if he was actually going for another piece of sushi or to grab me by the pussy.

My white knight snatched out like a ninja and grabbed the asshole by the wrist, twisting behind his back. The asshole started whining, "Ow, ow, ow!" But he didn't protest, not like you'd expect from some rich brat. No *"Do you have any idea who my uncle is?"* or *"You'll be hearing from my lawyer,"* or anything like that. I thought that was odd. He did say, "I was just getting a California roll," but that was it, and it was really apologetic.

Honestly, I was just so worried about them making a scene, that they'd get me fired, I didn't know what to do or say. I was actually starting to like this gig, in spite of the few oglers and the grabby asshole. If Eloise thought I was a troublemaker, she'd never hire me again.

My white knight snapped his fingers to get someone's attention, the ones not holding the asshole's hand behind his back. "There's a great new sushi place on Santa Monica, Braxton," my white knight says, holding the guy's eyes, not even breaking a sweat. "In fact, I think it's right on your way home, isn't it, Logan?"

The friend, Logan, I guess, nodded. My white knight didn't let the asshole answer, just shoved him away as two bodyguards in black suits came to escort him from my table. I didn't see what happened after that, since I couldn't turn my head to look.

"You okay?" my white knight asked. "Blink once for yes, twice for no." He grinned at me and I obliged him with a single blink and a smile. He didn't look super wealthy or anything, and it wasn't like I read Forbes or something, so I had no idea who he was. His tuxedo wasn't much nicer than the bodyguards' suits, but his teeth gave him away. They were whiter than his crisp white shirt, almost stark white against his perfectly even tan, like white out on a manilla envelope.

"You're the new girl," he said. His jaw was chiseled and his deep blue eyes held me pinned. Not that I could move even if I wanted to. "Sienna, is it?"

I told him my birth name, but I felt like he already knew it. Like he was just playing aloof.

"Right," he said, looking my legs up and down slowly, like he was studying them. It's hard to describe, but I've seen that look a lot. Like wondering if everything works down there, and what kind of positions he could twist me into.

I figured Eloise must've told him. Or, less likely, Hannah.

"Yes, I'm disabled," I said, before he could ask. "No, I can't feel anything below my waist. Yes, it does make it difficult to do 'Gangnam Style' at weddings, but I've learned to live with that."

He looked at me like I'd spoken a foreign language, which I guess I did, partly. He stammered. It was kind of cute, actually. I guess I was already hooked. He asked if Gangnam style was a martial art of some kind and for some reason I cracked up, like Julia Roberts reaching for the diamond necklace in *Pretty Woman*. I guess I'd been holding it in all night and it just got pent up. I wasn't faking it so he'd like me. I mean, I figured he was rich but it's not like I knew he was the host. And Bill and Tracy were—*are* —doing pretty well for themselves, like you probably already guessed from the kind of money I'm sure they offered you to bring me back.

"It's a dance," I told him, about Gangnam style.

And he said, "I'm not much of a dancer."

Then he smiled, and I smiled back. Some guy came over, completely missing the energy between us, and he reached past my white knight to get a tuna roll off my belly. He popped it into his mouth, chewed noisily, breathing through his nose as he glanced at the two of us, then walked off.

"I'm not supposed to talk much," I told my white knight after the noisy eater left.

"I'm not much of a talker, either," he said.

I laughed, and he smiled again.

"What are you doing later?" he asked me.

"Tonight?" I tried to look around to see where Hannah or Eloise were without moving my head. I already felt like I'd been talking too much and she'd noticed and come over to berate me, but I risked another comment. "Are you asking me out or are you worried my chair's gonna turn back into a pumpkin?"

This time he laughed. "I guess that'd make you Cinderolla," he said, which made me laugh again.

He was very easy with me, and most guys, most *people*, they either wanna ask you all kinds of questions about how you became disabled or they act like they don't see the chair at all, which is just as weird, if not worse.

"I was just thinking, you're quite statuesque," he said. "Have you ever done any runway modeling?"

"I did. Before my Little Act of God," I told him, gesturing toward my legs with my eyes.

"That's an interesting way to put it," he said.

And I said, "I'm an interesting girl."

He hummed and he nodded, then he reached out with his chopsticks for one of the *tsukemono* dishes beside my hip, the pickled vegetables, but instead of grabbing a piece of cucumber or carrot, he poked me in the hip. He wasn't smiling or taunting. It was like he was watching to see if I'd react.

"What the fuck?" I blurted out. The son of a bitch thought I was faking it. So I asked him that.

"I had my doubts," he admitted.

I honestly couldn't believe it. Even though we just met—and I didn't even know his name, I just realized in that moment—I thought we'd had a connection. He'd swooped in and saved me from the asshole and his friend, he'd been funny, we'd been funny together, and now this. Treating me like a science fair experiment. Like a human pincushion.

"Who would *fake* something like that?" I said. "And *why*?"

My white knight shrugged and asked, "Why does anyone do anything?"

That wasn't the sort of question I was used to answering, not at eighteen, but judging by who he was I had a feeling I already knew the answer. "You think I'm faking being disabled for money?" I asked.

"I've seen crazier things, believe me," he said. He raised his eyebrows at me and started walking away from my table, and that was that.

I thought it was the last time I'd see him, truthfully, and I actually thought he might try to get me fired. But the rest of the night went well, and when the band called for the host, my white knight took the stage. He was *billionaire bad-boy Nathan Rowan*. He didn't do much more than thank the people for coming, for eating his food and drinking his wine, he thanked them for their donations to the charity— whatever it was, and if I'd known I was going to end up seeing him again, let alone strike up a relationship with him, I might've filed it away in my memory— and then he left the stage. I think he even left the party.

No more jerks or weirdos that night, although the noisy eater came back two more times. Once all the party guests left, the nice chef with the scar removed the leftover sushi from our bodies and we even got to eat most of it. It was really good, even though some of it'd been sitting on me for over an hour.

On our way out, Eloise Delice thanked me and paid me in cash, and Hannah thanked me, said I should call her sometime. But it turned out Eloise wanted me to work more of these gigs so I'd end up seeing her anyway, just about once a week, sometimes more. *Nyotaimori* wasn't a big craze in L.A. back then, but as a side-hustle Eloise and her chef friend were making decent money, and so was I.

I'm a little thirsty, Michael, can we—?

"YEAH, SURE," Enhart said. "Want me to get you some water?"

Gloria shook her head lightly. "What I'd really like..." She shook her head again. "No," she said.

"What?" Enhart said, genuinely curious.

"Well," she started warily, "in the community, we're not allowed anything with artificial flavors."

Enhart couldn't help but grin. Could he really have chipped away at her that easily, gained her trust just sitting here listening to her, with barely any arguing at all? Somehow they'd zipped past the first four steps of his five-step program, and already got to the identification/transference stage, where the subject begins to identify with the deprogrammer.

After the last two members he'd pulled, it seemed these so-called Children of Dinah were easy nuts to crack. Almost like they were just waiting on any excuse to turn on their leader.

Gloria was a far cry from viewing Mother Amelia and the Children of Dinah as *The Enemy*, the actual *transference* part of step five. Still, it all seemed too easy.

But cults, aside from their sinister aspects, were ostensibly safe places to share stories, share *pain*, with like-minded people. Like group therapy, only with a cult leader in place of a therapist. Part of the appeal was finding some sort of meaning in their lives, and a sense of belonging, a sense of identity. It was a lot easier to find those things these days, especially online, with all of the little boxes people liked to put themselves in, defining themselves in progressively narrower niches, like Russian nesting dolls. Straight white cishet vegan cyclists for Palestine. Asian trans Republican cinephiles. Black furry polyamorous Jews for Jesus.

As Gloria had said about her disability, *like it defines them as a person*. As if all of these "special interest groups," and "communities" were homogenous.

A couple of decades ago these same people would've balked at being labelled, at being put in boxes. These days, the more labels you had the better. They collected them like trading cards, like kids chasing their Pokémons.

The times they are a-changin', Enhart thought, still grinning. "Want me to get you a pop?"

Gloria shrugged and nodded, her body seemingly at odds with her desires.

I know the feeling, he thought. "What kind?"

Her tongue flicked out, moistening her chapped lips. "If they have a Pibb, get that, please. If not, Dr. Pepper." She smiled. "I like how the spice tickles my nose." She wiggled her nose to demonstrate, reminding him of Elizabeth Mongomery from *Bewitched*, and he couldn't help but think just how goddamn cute this girl was.

She's also half your age, he chided himself. Get it together, Mike.

"I'll see what I can do," he said, and stood with a slight groan. "Don't go anywhere."

Gloria chuckled. "Where would I go?"

Enhart smiled and crossed the room. He felt like he was beginning to build a rapport with her now. This wasn't part of the Gospel of the Children of Dinah, their tenets or practices, but she seemed to want to tell him her story, which he wasn't about to balk at.

Don't look a gift horse in the mouth, he thought as he opened the door.

He turned back to Gloria as he stepped out onto the walk. She gave him a tight smile, and he returned it, then he closed the door behind himself, and headed for the vending machines near the motel offices.

WHEN THE DOOR CLOSED, Gloria sat up stiffly and scanned the room, looking for anything she could use to her advantage.

Things were going as well as could be expected, the noose tightening around Michael Enhart's neck an inch at a time. Unless he was a terrific actor, which his earlier tells had revealed he wasn't, he was starting to feel like they were becoming chummy, practically pair bonding. He was married, and happily, so his defenses would be a little harder to chip away at.

But all men were essentially the same. Sooner or later, he'd wear down and succumb to her "feminine wiles."

The bathroom visit had been a stroke of genius, completely improvised on her part. She'd felt him getting semi-erect against her back as he'd lugged her to the toilet, his cheeks reddening from embarrassment. It almost made her physically ill to think about, but she'd definitely done worse in her life. The Nathan Rowan story was tailormade to take advantage of that sort of weakness in him, similar to what Mother Amelia had done with the photograph and the priest back when she was still just a sister.

That phone call from Enhart's wife couldn't have

been better timed. He'd come back to the room looking chalky, like someone had just walked over his grave. She'd use that to her advantage, too.

Everything was falling neatly into place.

With luck on her side, he'd be willing to open that door and let her go free in less than a few hours, even without her three miracles.

If Mother Amelia wills it, Gloria thought.

And of course, She did.

ACTS

*   *   *

"They didn't have Pibb," Enhart said as he
returned to the room. "No Dr. Pepper, either."
He shrugged, crossing swiftly to the foot of the bed.
"Guess you're out of luck."

"I guess so," she said, sounding disappointed.
"What'd you get?"

"Pepsi." He held up the lukewarm can. "Hope
that's okay."

She shrugged. "I'll drink anything at this point as
long as it's got sugar and all kinds of artificial crap."

Enhart went around to the chair. He popped the
top and held out the can to her. She took it, her eyes
dazzling as she brought it to her lips and guzzled. She
practically moaned in pleasure.

"That's really good!"

He sat in the chair, opening the second can for
himself. "I'm a Diet Coke guy, myself. But I'll usually
drink Pepsi in a pinch." He held it up in a toast. "To
artificial crap."

"To artificial crap," she repeated, raising her own.

They each sipped their Pepsis.

"I guess you'd probably get in big trouble if

Mother Amelia found out you were doing this," he said after a moment of drawn-out silence.

"You have no idea."

He grinned. "I have *some* idea. My wife, Christie-Ann, she'd kill me if she knew I drank this stuff. Or ate the burger and fries I had before I went and got you."

Gloria took another healthy swig. "Oh yeah? Why's that?"

"Well, she's a real health nut. Sometimes I feel like she's got me on a cult diet herself."

"That's funny."

"How so?"

"Well, that's kind of where my story about Nathan Rowan was going. Sometimes relationships feel like a cult, don't you think? Cults of two. A sort of a *folie à deux*, only instead of a shared delusion, it's a mutual obsession with each other. When you think about it, delusions and obsessions share a fair amount of commonalities."

He took another sip. "In what sense?"

"Well, they both affect your ability to function in everyday life, don't they? Then there's the inability to stop yourself from thinking about your obsession pretty much whenever, whether it's a thing or a fetish or another person."

"Or revenge, like your Mother Amelia."

"Right," she said, and held his gaze. "Like, there are some obvious big differences. And depending on the obsession, it's usually a whole lot less dangerous than most delusions can get. Still, you can't deny the similarities."

Enhart thought about it. He wasn't sure he agreed, but at this stage in the game it was good to be agreeable. "Yeah, I guess so," he said.

"That's what I had with Nathan, anyway, and what I thought he had with me. Despite the stupid thing with the chopsticks, I couldn't help but think about him as I lay in bed that night."

Gloria looked over at him and caught his eye. Enhart held her gaze for a moment, then looked down at his pop. His throat clicked audibly as he swallowed, trying not to think about her lying under the covers, all by herself, fantasizing about this guy. Did she still masturbate, in her condition? Could she even have orgasms?

She was still watching him, seeming to study his expression. He took another sip from his can to cover as his cheeks began to burn again.

"He called my house later that week," she said, continuing her story.

WELL, his secretary did. People still had home phones back then, not like now. Tracy answered the call. I was in the kitchen with her, fixing my lunch, about to roll my way back out to the pool to eat. I saw her eyes pop out of her head just like Eloise's when she first saw my chair. Then she said, almost robotically flat, "All right. I'll tell her. Okay, thank you. Goodbye."

After that she hung up and just looked at me until I couldn't take it anymore.

"What?" I asked. At first, I thought maybe it was my physio doctor's office with an appointment reminder. Judging by her initial reaction, I wondered if maybe it was my surgeon calling to try some new experimental surgery so I could walk again and she was trying to play it cool.

Finally, she says, "That was Nathan Rowan's office. Why would Nathan Rowan's office be calling you?"

"His *office*?" I said, because first of all why would he be calling me, and second, why wouldn't he call me *himself*?

Tracy nodded. "Apparently he wants you to meet him there tomorrow. Eleven sharp, his secretary said."

"Why would he want me to meet him there?"

"*Does it matter?*" she said. "It's *Nathan Rowan*." Like that said it all. Like she would've sold me off to him for two goats and a shack if she could've, but she already had her eyes set on a summer home in the Florida Keys.

So I told her I'd have to think about it. I mean, he was hot, don't get me wrong. He'd saved me from that giant douchebag and his friend. But he'd also been a bit cocky. And then there was the thing with the chopstick in the hip assuming I was faking it.

What could he want with me?

After dinner, after Tracy related the story—brief as it was—to Bill, we talked about it for a bit and I agreed I would go. Just to see what he wanted. It felt like the beginning of one of those billionaire romance novels I'd been reading all summer, to be honest, but I didn't want to a) get my hopes up, or b) go there under the wrong impression.

Like maybe he wanted an intern and needed to fill some diversity quota? Or maybe, since he did ask about my modeling days, he was hosting another charity event and he wanted a model who'd "challenge standard norms of beauty." In other words, I'd have to learn how to catwalk in my chair. That sort of inclusionary stuff was already becoming normalized in the beauty industry at that time, but it wasn't prevalent yet. I didn't have any grand ideas about being the

Rosa Parks of disabled models, but I was sort of mulling over thoughts about what my life would be like if I was able to go back to modeling. *Real* modeling, not the body sushi stuff.

But I was getting ahead of myself. And it turned out it was neither of those things.

What Nathan Rowan wanted was more complicated than all that.

The next morning, Tracy drove me to the Hurlitzer building in the Financial District, and somehow we managed to get lucky with L.A. traffic and got there twenty minutes earlier than I expected. While Tracy drove around to find parking, I went up to his office myself. When I got to his floor, a young guy who was going in at the same time held the door for me. Bill had told me what Rowan Enterprises did, but my eyes glazed over as soon as he started talking about hedge funds and all that. From the look of the guy, he was what they call a "finance bro" these days. I was wearing a cute little black dress with black stockings to cover up the scars on my legs, and I was looking good. So I wasn't surprised and didn't feel self-conscious when he very obviously checked me out.

Nathan's secretary greeted me. She said he was in a meeting. She was nice but curt. An older woman, not unattractive, but not a smokeshow like Eloise Delice. I think she might've been wary of her boss's intentions for me. She did this thing with raising just her left eyebrow like she was dubious of everything I did. Like she thought I was faking it like her boss did the other night at the party. Or maybe she was worried he was grooming me to take over her job. As it turned out, I never had to worry about that.

While I waited, I could see his silhouette pacing back and forth behind the frosted glass of his inner office door. He kept me waiting until exactly eleven, then he buzzed the intercom.

"Send her in, please, Frieda," he said.

So the secretary, Frieda, got up and opened the door for me, with her trademark eyebrow raise. Nathan was standing beside one of those golf putter things. As I rolled in, he took the shot, or whatever you call it, and got a hole in one. He bent to pick up the ball, and I felt like he was deliberately showing off his butt in his Tom Ford stretch wool dress pants.

He was sexy and he knew it, and knew that I knew it. He looked up at me and caught my eye as my eyes snapped up from checking him out, and he flashed me his million-dollar smile. *Billion*-dollar smile, technically.

The internet said he was twenty-eight when I looked him up after I went up to bed the night before. That made him almost a decade older than me. But it wouldn't be the first time an older guy took an interest.

"Thanks for coming," he said. "I was worried you wouldn't show."

"I was curious," I said.

"Curious?"

He sat on the edge of his desk and gestured for me to join him. I crossed the room, but not too close. I didn't want him to think he'd hooked me that soon, especially after the chopstick incident.

"I wondered what a thirty-year-old hedge fund billionaire might want with a crippled Orange County girl, fresh out of high school."

He laughed. "Not thirty just yet, thanks." He reached for a humidor beside him and picked out a cigar. "Mind if I smoke?"

"I'd prefer if you didn't," I said. I don't mind cigar

smoke. Jackson used to roll blunts with those flavored cigars, and I got used to the smell of them. I just wanted him to have to play on my rules.

He smiled again and closed the box. "I asked you to join me this morning because... well, I thought we hit it off the other night, Savannah. And I feel like you and I have an interesting perspective on life most people, especially in my circles, just don't seem to get."

"Oh really?" I said. "What perspective is that?"

He looked surprised, like I should've known exactly what he meant. Like our perspectives were so in line I should've just been able to read his mind. Like our periods were in sync or something.

"We've *cheated death*," he said, and he picked up some kind of crystal paperweight off the desk, mesmerized by it as he twirled it back and forth in his fingers. It caught the sunlight from the window wall—I forgot to mention the view, which was amazing and kind of scary—and when the light flashed in my eyes for a second, just about blinding me, I had an image of him pushing me up against the glass and fucking my brains out for the whole city to see.

"Oh," I said, swallowing a lump in my throat. I'd read about his skiing accident at Heavenly Mountain, and that he almost died. He'd fractured his spine and broken seven or eight bones, not including his ribs. The doctors said he might never walk again. But then, after a year or two of physiotherapy, the articles said he'd had a miraculous recovery.

"Our little Acts of God," he said with a grin, placing the paperweight or whatever it was back on the desk.

"Right."

He tented his fingers under his chin. "Am I making you uncomfortable?"

"No, I'm totally—" I stopped myself, realizing I was starting to sound like the teenager I was, though by then I felt like I'd lived through so much already that my peers felt like children. He was right, about our perspectives. When you come that close to dying, it changes you, especially if you aren't able to come all the way back like me.

Nathan Rowan sprang back, and then some. He was the head of a billion-dollar hedge fund management firm. Sure, it was his father's business, but he was on Forbes' 30 Under 30 list just that past year. He was a *superstar* in the finance world. A *wunderkind*, people were calling him. And I was some high school grad who couldn't even strike up the courage to swim in her own backyard pool.

"Yes, you are making me uncomfortable," I admitted, my cheeks burning. "I don't know what you want from me. Okay, so we both nearly died. But there's a big difference, isn't there? You can walk. You got to dance at your own prom. You're also richer than I could ever even possibly dream of. My entire house could probably fit in your bathroom."

He chuckled. "I get it. You're intimidated. You see a man like me and you think, 'What could he possibly need in his life that I could give him?' So I won't tiptoe around it, no pun intended. I'll tell you."

And then he did. There was a performance artist, he told me, this woman who stood in art spaces and let people touch her, write on her with markers, use knives and whips and chains on her body. Nathan's parents took him to one of her performances when he was four years old, back when she was still touring this particular "piece," if you can call it that. His parents didn't know what type of performance it was going to be, just that she was the "next big thing," according to their friends in the art world, and his mother was deep into art in those days, especially art that challenged norms. And he watched, this poor little four-year-old boy, as people—mostly men, but some women, too—slapped and pinched and prodded this artist's naked body. Choked her. Hit her with chains. Struck her with the whip. Cut her with the knives. Her whole body was already covered with scars from the other performances, and there were Polaroids of those instances of violence against her spread out all over the table behind her, almost as a challenge. To give these people permission to use her as "art."

"You've got to be fucking kidding me," I said.

He smiled, sadly this time, and shook his head. "I want you to be my canvas, Savannah," he said. He pulled his shirt out of his pants and showed me his own scars, pale ones that stood out against his taut abs and the dark trail of hair leading down below his navel as starkly as the smile on his face. But he wasn't smiling now.

"I can't do it to myself anymore," he told me, studying me while I stared at his V-cut abs. Then he laughed. "I can't take the pain, if you can believe that."

I ogled his body for a long moment, trying to catch my breath. I suddenly felt like I was hyperventilating. My cheeks were hot. He wanted me to... let him *abuse* me?

"You've gotta be fucking kidding me," I said again. It was just about all I could *think* to say.

"I'll give you whatever you want, Savannah," he told me then, *pinning* me with his eyes as he tucked his shirt back into his pants. "You want a nice car, I'll get you a car. A house in Beverly Hills for you and your parents? It's yours. When I say 'money is no object,' Savannah, I don't mean it like when your boyfriend takes you out to Ruth's Chris Steak House on Valentine's Day. Money is literally not my concern." He laid the crystal thing back on his desk. "I want *you*, Savannah," he told me. "I *need* you."

ENHART'S PHONE BUZZED, interrupting her story.

He'd been sitting on the edge of his seat, and the phone buzzing under his ass nearly made him jump out of it.

"Jesus," he muttered. He reached into his back pocket, slipped out the phone, and read the text.

Jessa's in surgery now! Wish us luck! Love you!!

THEY'D NAMED her Jessa after Christie-Ann's mother. Enhart had never met the woman, nor had he met her father. They'd died years before he met Christie-Ann in that truck stop diner in Buckhannon, Virginia.

Gloria asked him something as he stared at the phone.

"Huh?" he said.

"I said, 'Is something wrong?'"

Could he confide in her this early? Tit for tat was one thing but to truly open up about deeply private matters....

Dad sure wouldn't've approved, he thought.

"It's fine," he lied, trying to even out his heartrate and his breathing. He typed up a quick text—*Good luck! Love you too, Bunches!*—and fired it off. Then he set the phone on the bedside table.

"Where were we?"

"Nathan just told me he needed me."

"Right." Enhart glanced at the phone.

Gloria frowned at him. "Are you sure you're okay?"

He nodded. Only he wasn't okay. He was far from okay. How could he focus on her story when his mind was on Jessa?

He *needed* to focus. To be attentive, able to respond when required and ask pertinent questions. It was his *job*. It was what her mother was *paying him* to do. He needed to seem like he cared when all he could think about was his kid going under the knife, a little girl born three pounds and fifteen ounces, who cried and screamed more than she slept and who'd almost felt like a burden, if he were being truly honest with himself, up until just about an hour ago.

He glanced at the phone again, expecting it to buzz with another text from Christie-Ann, and took an anxious sip from the nearly empty can.

Focus, Mike. The surgeon's got this in hand. You just need to get your head back in the game.

It was easier said than done. His dad used to tell him time and time again, *You can't let your personal life interfere with the job, son.* Up until he'd met Christie-Ann, that'd never been an issue. Even then, he'd easily been able to separate his home life from work. Christie-Ann hadn't demanded much of his time. She waited on his nightly calls, when he was able to get away, but she didn't fuss if he missed one night, and she rarely if ever called him, unless it was an emergency. Aside from her weird obsession with fad diets, she was just about the least demanding woman he'd ever met.

But now, he was a father himself. He had more than just one person to be accountable for. He should be there with them, not in some sleazy motel listening to a stranger tell stories of people he didn't care about. He should've pushed this job forward the minute he'd found out Christie-Ann's placenta had separated.

At least I was there for the birth. I'm not that much like him. We need a miracle right now. A real miracle. Not one of Gloria's stories.

But the wheels were already in motion. The only way to get back to his wife and child was to keep pushing gently forward. Listen to Gloria's stories. Push back. Win her over to his side. *Their* side.

It was the stories that'd drawn him to this job initially, even though he'd essentially inherited the family business, and veteran deprogrammer Bob Ingles along with it. He needed to remember that, now more than ever. When these people finally opened up to him, revealed their failed dreams and hidden shames, he found the entire process cathartic, both for himself and the victim.

He'd always been a good listener. When he was little, he'd sat and listened to his mom and the others in the community sharing their stories. They'd always told him what a "good little listener" he'd been. What a "quiet, attentive boy" he was. They'd always seemed so happy when they said these things to him, and seeing them happy, his mother especially, had made him happy.

His dad had only ever talked to him to scold him or to teach him things, often both at the same time. How to be a good man. How to be a father, as if he'd been the paragon of fatherhood himself. How to do his job and do it well.

True to his nature, Michael Enhart had listened.

He'd always thought, in another life, if he hadn't been such a dumb palooka, screwing around so much in high school, he'd have made a good therapist.

But even the best therapists had therapists of their own. They were modern-day sin-eaters, absorbing the transgressions and traumas and stresses of others and offering thoughts and advice. They needed someone to confide in themselves, to unburden themselves of their own pain and secrets. Enhart confided in Christie-Ann. She listened well and provided good feedback. She *grounded* him. He'd become infinitely better at his job since he'd met her. He was truly lucky to have her.

His father had no one after his divorce, long before he'd separated Enhart from his mother. Eventually, the weight of the sins he'd eaten over the years had been too much for him to bear.

This will be okay, Enhart thought, conjuring up a memory of Christie-Ann touching his cheek, tilting her head, offering him a sympathetic smile.

"Yeah," he said, exhaling sharply through his nose. "I'll be fine."

Gloria held his gaze a moment longer, nodded as if she wasn't sure she believed him, then continued her story.

FOLLY

N athan wanted me, or he wanted my body at
    least, and he wasn't ready to take no for an
answer.

"I don't have a boyfriend," I told him.

He looked at me like I grew three heads. He'd just
revealed his deepest, darkest desires to me and the
thing I thought to respond to was about the steak
house on Valentine's Day. I was kind of stunned myself. "What?" he said.

"He died in the crash. Instantly, they said. Same
with Pearl. Davis was burned alive while I lay on the
side of the road, unable to move."

"I'm sorry," he said. "I didn't know—"

"No, you didn't. We're not the same, Nathan. You
fractured your spine in a skiing accident. You were
with family and friends who got you to the hospital in
a helicopter. I listened to my best friend's boyfriend
scream in agony as he *burned to death* in front of me,
and I couldn't do *a thing* to help him." I rolled right
up to him, just to put the point across. "And now you
can walk, and I'm stuck in this fucking chair!"

As I said it, I reached out and swiped the heavy

crystal thing off his desk. It hit the floor at his feet, but it didn't break. I wished it'd broken. It would've been a perfect underscore for the point I was trying to get across, and it seemed sentimental to him. I really wanted to hurt him right then.

Nathan looked down at the paperweight, then at me, not with anger or pity, not even with sympathy. I don't think he really thought of me as another person at all. I was a blank canvas to him, like the performance artist he'd seen when he was still too young and impressionable to understand what consent means.

"You want to walk again?" he said finally, pulling up his pantlegs and crouching to pick it up. He looked up at me with it in his hand. "I can't promise you that, but I *can* say the best spinal surgeons in the world are right at my fingertips. I'll gladly pay for whatever surgeries you need to make your wish come true. Be my muse, Savannah. Please don't make me beg you."

"Why not?" I shot back. "You're already so close to getting down on your knees."

He chuckled lightly, placed the paperweight gently back on the desk, then got down on both knees. He looked up at me with puppy dog eyes, his hands together like a prayer. "Please, Savannah," he said. "I have the whole world to give you, but it's nothing compared to what you can give to me."

I never understood the phrase "I melted" until just that moment. He was gorgeous. He was rich. He was broken. It was just like those books I'd been reading, or at least it was in my head. I don't imagine you've read any, but in those books the bad-boy billionaire keeps his pain carefully concealed. It's only revealed during the course of their relationship as the MC—the main character—gets him to open up.

I never found that part sexy, to be honest. I tend to gravitate toward strong men who aren't afraid to be vulnerable, who aren't afraid to cry. They know how to be soft, and when it's time to be hard.

Nathan Rowan had shown me all of that in two brief interactions. How could I *not* give him what he wanted? What he *needed*? How could I be so callous to deprive him of that?

So I said yes. Obviously, we couldn't do whatever it was he wanted from me right there in his office, so he told me he'd bring a car around to pick me up that night if I didn't already have plans. Fortunately, I wasn't doing a sushi gig so I said yes again. By then I was starting to wonder if I'd say yes to just about anything he asked, but I told myself I could say no any time I wanted. He'd asked for my consent, after all.

The "car," according to what Bill told me later, was a 1977 Rolls Royce Phantom VI. Bill said it was a limousine, but it wasn't as long as the ones I'm used to, like the kind kids rent for prom. All I knew was that it looked like it was made long before I was born, but it was so shiny it could've come right off the line. The driver helped me into the backseat and collapsed my chair to put it in the trunk.

His name was Alphonse, but I was to call him Al. "Like the song," I said, and he half grinned. That's about all I got out of him. I asked him some questions about Nathan, about how long he'd worked for him. Pretty much one-word answers. The strong, silent type, like they used to say. He drove me up to Nathan's palatial estate where Nathan stood waiting for me, leaning against the frame of the front doors with his hands in the pockets of his white linen pants and his legs crossed casually at the ankles.

"Thank you for coming," he said, coming down to

meet me. Alphonse got my chair out of the trunk and Nathan rolled it over. I was wearing a nice summery dress that showed off my legs and my shoulders. I saw him lick his lips as he got a glimpse of my thighs when I shifted from the backseat into the chair.

He grabbed the handles and wheeled me around.

"I can do it," I said.

"Of course you can," he said. "You can do anything you put your mind to, Savannah."

I got the feeling he was teasing me. "Everything except walk across your threshold."

He half-shrugged. "Not yet," he said. "That reminds me, I went ahead and booked a consult for you with my orthopedic surgeon. I hope you don't mind."

"Why would I mind?" I asked, rolling up to the house. "That's why I'm here, isn't it?"

"Right," he said, walking alongside me. "I've also drawn up a contract. Nothing too complicated. It's just to protect you legally if you decide all of this is too much for you, and you need to quit."

"I'm a strong girl."

He smiled down at me. "I know that, Savannah. That's why I chose you."

He gave me a brief tour of the house, showing me rooms and art and furniture I'd never gotten a chance to see the last time I was here. Even still, the place seemed different, and I mentioned that.

"Good eye," he said. "I had some things moved out for the event. Some of this art is priceless, and I don't like to flaunt my wealth *too* much, if you know what I mean."

"Yeah, that's the first thing I noticed about you, actually," I said. "I said to myself, this guy doesn't nearly look rich enough."

He grinned. "Plus, a lot of this is from my mother's decorator," he explained. "Not quite to my taste, but I keep it out just in case she drops by."

"Does she drop by unannounced a lot?"

"Here and there," he said, nodding. He stopped in front of a door on the second floor at the back of the east wing. It was no different than any of the others, aside from the fact that it had a padlock on it. "Here's where we'll be spending most of your time with me," he said, pulling out a set of keys from his right pocket and using one on the lock.

"Is this your 'playroom'?" I asked, using the term Christian Grey has for his sex dungeon in *Fifty Shades*.

Nathan glanced back at me with a look in his eyes I couldn't decipher. "It's my atelier," he told me. "My art studio."

Then he opened the door.

True to his word, it really was a studio. There were paintings on easels and stacked up against the walls, dozens of them. One of them, on another easel, was covered by a cloth.

"I didn't know you painted," I said. The ones visible were very different than anything else in the house. Later on, he described his style as "a clash of Modigliani and Francis Bacon." I had to look them up, and I could definitely see the influence. They were filled with elongated figures, grotesque faces and body parts. The only real difference was, his weren't any good. Even I could tell that, and I'd only taken art up until the tenth grade. Still, because of who he was, he probably could've sold them for a pretty penny.

"I dabble," he said self-consciously. "Not as much as I used to before I took over the company. No time."

"They're good," I lied.

"Sweet of you to lie," he said. "I know they're no

good. But I like to paint. My father always called it 'Nathan's Folly.'"

"That's not very nice."

"He wasn't a very nice man. My mother has a kinder way to tell me they're crap. She just says they 'don't go with the décor.'"

"So," I said with a smirk, "are you planning to paint me like one of your French girls?"

I really hoped the answer was no, because despite what I *thought* he wanted from me, I really didn't want to see what I'd look like with a horse face and long, spindly legs that looked like raw steak.

"No, Savannah," he said, unsmiling.

In the middle of the room was another large drop cloth spread out under a worktable. "Come," he said, crossing to it. I followed him to the table, where a stack of papers waited for us. He picked them up and held them out for me.

It was a contract, like he'd said, written in a bunch of legalese I didn't understand. *I (blank), hereafter referred to as The Canvas, agree to blah blah blah.*

"The Canvas?" I asked, already confused by all the lawyer-speak. "Is this for real?"

He fixed me with a penetrating look. "It's just for your protection, as I said. Have your lawyer take a look at it, if you like. We can wait."

I didn't want to wait. I wanted it to be over and done with. I wanted to walk again. So I glanced through it, and from what I understood it gave me certain rights about pulling out of the deal and gave him certain rights indemnifying him from me suing for abuse or assault. It was basically a consent form for BDSM, and since I was consenting, I signed it.

"Good," he said, smiling. "Let's get started."

He had me get up on the table—it was a little

higher than I'm used to so he helped me up—and lie down flat on my back. Then he ran his fingertips lightly over my legs, over the raised scars, admiring them. Even though I couldn't feel it, there was a sensuousness to his touch and his gaze that turned me on.

"You're perfect," he told me.

No one had ever called me *perfect* before. People don't use that word in the modeling world, and if they do you know they literally say it to all the girls. Even Jackson never called me *perfect*.

He started slowly, striking my calves with a cat o' nine tails. Lightly at first, methodically. His eyes darting back and forth from the red marks he was making to my eyes. I wondered if he still thought I was faking it.

"Can you roll over, please?" he asked.

I obliged him, and he started striking the backs of my legs. Once, twice, three times. He flinched himself on the last two, but I still felt nothing, of course. I knew I'd have some pretty bad welts I'd have to explain when I got home, so I'd smartly brought a pair of tights to wear to cover up any marks.

I was looking over my shoulder when he flipped up the back of my dress, revealing the white silk panties I wore for two reasons: one, if he had a bit of a schoolgirl thing, which was just a guess because of our age gap, I knew he'd prefer these over thongs. And two, my doctor said I shouldn't wear thongs for hygiene reasons. Not to be gross, but if i get any kind of infection down there it's not like I'd feel it.

"Perfect," he said again. He bit his lower lip as he stared at my ass—I made the right choice with the panties, I guess—and began whipping me. Softly at first, then harder and harder. Just a couple of inches higher and I would've felt it, but where he was hitting me I had no sensation at all.

After a while he shuddered and his eyes kind of went blank as he stared off toward the closed door. I noticed a bit of blood had seeped through the white fabric. He'd hit me at least one time hard enough to break the skin.

He took a few pictures with a Polaroid camera, then he said, "We're done for today. I'll walk you out."

It was a little abrupt, and as he helped me into my chair I couldn't help but think he felt guilty for what he'd done to me.

I wanted to ask, *Who did this to you?* It couldn't *just* be that performance piece all those years ago, could it? Would a thing like that fuck someone up for that long?

We didn't speak the whole way back. There were so many things I wanted to say, to ask him, but I couldn't bring myself to do it and I didn't know what to ask first. When we got to the car, I finally got up the guts to ask when I should I expect a call from the surgeon.

He looked annoyed, and he didn't meet my gaze when he replied. "He's booked up solid for the next little while, but I was able to book you in for a couple of weeks from now."

"Great," I said. "Thank you."

His demeanor changed like that. He smiled down at me and squeezed my shoulder. It was the first touch of his I'd felt, firm yet gentle. It made my spine tingle at the nape of my neck.

"Thank *you*, my muse," he said.

God, I wanted him.

When I got home, I iced all my fresh welts and wounds. The one of my left cheek was the worst, the one that bled into my underwear. I applied ointment to it, and a bandage. The bed sores I got in the hospital made me wary of open wounds, especially on my backside, where I usually slept.

Frieda called me the next day, sounding annoyed. She said Nathan was on a brief business trip but wanted to see me in two days. The wounds were already healing, so I said why not?

Two days later, he was waiting for me, leaning against the door frame like before.

I'd taken off my tights in the car, the ones I wore to hide the fresh welts and bruises from Bill and Tracy, and was wearing a tennis skirt with bare legs. He looked at them with clear disappointment in his gaze.

"What happened?" he demanded.

I asked him what he meant.

"The welts are gone," he said.

I told him I iced the welts and bruises and used ointment on the one on my butt.

He looked at me firmly. "Next time, don't do that," he said.

We went back to his workshop then, but this time the table was moved out of the way and there were leather cuffs on shackles hanging from the ceiling above the drop cloth.

Back in the hospital, after my accident, they had me hang from bars as part of my physio. It was a body harness, not cuffs, and I had a walker to hold on to, but it still gave me flashbacks.

"You're nervous," he said.

"What gave that away?"

He smirked. "You can back out any time you want to, Savannah. Just say the word."

"Which word?" I asked.

"You tell me," he said.

"We should have a safe word, shouldn't we?"

"Safe word?" He raised an eyebrow. For a minute there, it reminded me of Frieda, his secretary.

"You know. Like BDSM," I said.

"This isn't sexual, Savannah." His tone and facial expression were deadly serious.

"I know," I said, though I wondered if like Lady Macbeth maybe he was protesting a bit too much. "But maybe we should have one. In case it gets too much for me."

He smirked. "How about 'Rosebud'?"

"Rosebud?"

"Like the movie," he said. When I didn't clue in fast enough for him, he said, "*Citizen Kane*?"

"Right. Rosebud it is."

With the safe word decided, I rolled over to the shackles and Nathan strapped my wrists in, then began hoisting me to my feet. He locked off the chains and I stood suspended by my wrists with my toes grazing the floor. But since my feet were useless, all of my weight was on my arms. It was uncomfortable, but I thought I could hold it as long as he wasn't planning to keep me like this forever.

He repeated what he'd done last time with the cat o' nine tails, only now I was vertical. I guess this was what he'd been leading up to, because the performance artist had been shackled the same way in his story, though I imagine she wasn't a paraplegic, allowing her feet to bear some of her weight.

"Tell me your greatest fear," he said, and flogged me just below my ass.

"Why?" I asked.

"Revealing our fears is freeing, isn't it? Not spiders or heights or silly things like that. I mean your truest, deepest fear."

I told him. Sometimes I worry I'll move the wrong way and my spine will crack further up and I'll be paralyzed from the neck down, unable to move my arms or my neck, and I'll have to go to the bathroom in bags and blink to communicate. I still wake up some nights dreaming about that.

"Like *Johnny Got His Gun*," he said. "That's horrifying."

"What about you?" I asked. "What's your deepest fear?"

Rather than reply, he struck me on the small of my back. It stung, and I hissed in a breath. I wasn't sure if he'd meant to hit me above the hips but when I looked back at him his eyes were manic. The hairs on the back of my neck stood up.

The thing was, I kind of *liked* it. Jackson used to pull my hair when we fucked. Not too hard, just enough so it stung a bit. I'd bite his neck and we rutted like animals. So when the whip stung me and I felt a sort of tingle between my legs, I just about lost my mind.

It'd been so long since I felt anything down there, and believe me, I tried. Using my hand didn't get me anywhere. I even tried one of those Hitachi wands when someone suggested it on a message board. Nada. Zero sensation.

So when I felt my pussy getting hot on the next strike, I guess I must've moaned without knowing it, because he started whipping up higher on my back, which got me even hotter.

I looked back to see him biting his lip as he hit me. It was obvious how hard I made him through his loose-fitting slacks.

And then it happened. It just sort of washed over me like a wave, and I screamed, "*Rosebud!*" while cumming so hard I couldn't hold myself up by my arms any longer, and I just sort of hung there like a slab of meat on a hook with everything above my waist quivering for what seemed like minutes, while Nathan snapped photos with the Polaroid.

Then he rolled my chair over, pushed it up behind me, and uncuffed me. I slumped into my chair, exhausted.

"We're done for today," he said. His face was flushed and the tent in his pants was still pitched. I wanted so badly to reach out and grab it, to take him into my mouth, to please him as he'd pleased me, but I still wasn't sure that was what he wanted from me. What if he rejected me? What if he threw me out? Or worse: what if he pulled out of the contract and I didn't get a chance to see his surgeon?

We went on like this for a couple of weeks, sometimes in the shackles, sometimes on the table. Each time I got even more sure he was orgasming along with me, just shooting huge ropes of cum into his boxers. I wanted to taste him so badly, but I couldn't bring myself to say anything or do anything and by the time I thought I'd worked up the courage he'd already taken his photos and said, "We're done for today."

It was maybe a month in, waiting out front for the car, when he asked me if I was free the following night. I told him I had a body sushi gig, which was a lie. I'd lost the body sushi job a few weeks earlier when Eloise freaked out over all of my new scars and welts. But I didn't want to look like I was too eager, so I told him the next night I was available.

He considered it, then agreed. "Dinner, not a session," he told me.

I smirked. "What, like a date?"

He gave me a hard look. "Not like a date, Savannah. I want you to meet my mother."

His *mother*? Why would he want *me* to meet his mother?

That's what bothered me that night, terrified me while I was getting ready. What was this about? What should I wear? I didn't want his mom to think I looked like a little high school trollop, but I didn't want to *overdress* for her either. Finally, I settled on a summery, sleeveless maxi dress, and a good pair of chunky heels, which were in fashion at the time.

His mother turned out to be none other than Frieda, although she was dressed elegantly instead of her demure business attire. Apparently, she'd been his father's secretary before they married and just never stopped doing it. When Nathan took over after his father died, she stayed on. And her patented eyebrow raises were flowing freely the more wine was poured. It was obvious she didn't like me right from the get-go, or at least didn't like what me being there meant about her son, and she made that dislike painfully clear throughout what was otherwise a lovely dinner.

"*She's eighteen years old*, Nathan," she said at one point.

"She's *my muse*, mother," he said, practically whining.

I was embarrassed. It was a side of him I didn't like to see, but I told myself everybody has weird things with their parents, like me with Tracy, and just tried my best not to get too drunk with all of my awkward drinking and eating.

Well, about halfway through, Nathan got a call and had to leave us alone.

The two of us sat there awkwardly for a bit after

he left. Then Frieda said, "I'm not a horrible woman, you know. I'm doing my best to protect you."

"Protect me from what?" I asked, defensive.

"From Nathan's Folly," she said. That same phrase Nathan's dad used to use about his art. "May I show you something?"

She took me upstairs, to the west wing not the east, not saying a word to me the entire time but sort of drunkenly sashaying down the hall and humming Barbra Streisand's "The Way We Were." By the time we reached the equivalent of the door to his atelier, his art studio, I realized it was just a mirrored version of the east wing, only with different art. Frieda took a key out of her clutch purse and opened the door.

"Do you see?" she said, holding the door open for me.

The room was much smaller, the size of a darkroom, and there were little white and dark squares pinned all over the walls.

It was Polaroids. *Hundreds* of them.

He'd only taken maybe a dozen with me. And there must've been at least a dozen women in the photos, maybe way more. Pouting lips, sad eyes, runny mascara, raised welts and angry red scars. In the middle of all this were older Polaroids of a woman I recognized, sort of Eastern-European-looking and from the 1980s, a face I'd seen recently after verifying Nathan's story that first day. It was the performance artist from all those years ago, the one he'd seen when he was five. He must've bought up all her originals.

"So you see?" Frieda said. "You're just another in a long line of his 'muses.' Nathan's Folly was never his art. It was *confusing inspiration with love*."

I put on a brave face. It was either that or cry, which is what I wanted to do. I told her he showed me all of this already—which of course he hadn't—and that I only care about his art. And I told *myself* what I really cared about was walking again. Even though I knew that wasn't true.

I *liked* him.

And his mother had just basically told me he *loved me*.

She got Alphonse to pull the car around and drive me home. A couple of days passed without a call from her—she'd always set up my dates with Nathan, if he hadn't during our "session"—and I started to think she'd convinced him I was no good, that I was just in it for the money, etcetera.

Three days later, Nathan called me himself. Said he "needed to see me."

This is it, I thought. *We're breaking up.*

But when I got there, he treated it just like any other visit, leaning casually against the doorframe, leading me up to the art room, helping me onto the table. As if nothing had changed between us since the last time.

But things *had* changed. I'd met his mother. And she'd shown me his trophy room, his secret shame.

It was impossible *not* to see how hard I made him this time in the gray sweatpants he had on. His cock was practically pointing right at my face, and I knew I had to make a move. I had to be sure.

So while he whipped my legs, I pulled down my top so my tits stuck out of the halter. He just stared stupidly at them for several seconds, then used the whip on my nipples. With his attention on my tits, I jerked down his sweatpants and grabbed his shaft.

"Come," I said, pumping his rock-hard dick as he whipped me to orgasm.

When we came together it was like he'd been holding it back for months. Porn stars wished they could cum that hard. The first spurt shot past my head and over the table. The next ones hit me on the chin, the throat and plastered my tits. I wanted so badly to *taste* him, so I wiped some off my chin as he stood there shuddering the way I had that first day in the cuffs, and licked it off my hand like melted ice cream.

He stared at me, transfixed, for a long time. Then, when I thought he'd say something nice about how I'd made him cum so hard, he said, "We're done for today," just like every time before it. Then he grabbed a paint-streaked towel off the worktable and tossed it at me.

I sat up, pulling up my top despite my tits covered in his jizz, and I whipped the towel right back at him. It hit the back of his head and he still wouldn't turn around to look at me.

"'We're done for today'?" I snapped. "That's really all you have to say to me?"

He was moving his paints around on the work-table all OCD when he said, "Get out of my house," almost too quiet for me to hear. So I lost it on him.

"Your mother showed me your trophy room," I practically screamed at him. "This isn't about me *or* about art, is it? You're *getting off* on this shit from the Nineteen-fucking-Eighties!"

He turned to me then, jaw set and pointing at the door. "*Get. The fuck. Out of my house!*"

I just sat there on the table, arms crossed. He stomped over and grabbed my arms, picked me up while I fought against him, and sat me in my chair. Then he started rolling me to the door with his cum still dripping off me.

"We're done," he said, and shoved me down the hall.

I rolled on for a bit before braking and turning back. "What do you mean, 'we're done'? It's over? You said you *need* me! You said I was *perfect*!"

"You're not perfect, Savannah," he said. He was blank-faced and his tone was flat. "You're just like the others."

I felt a tear spill down my cheek. I hadn't felt this awful since my Little Act of God. "I'll sue," I said.

He laughed. He *actually laughed* at me. Then he said the contract was never legally binding for either of us. He said you can't legally consent to torture.

I told him I'd go to the police.

"Be my guest," he said. "Walk right up to the police station—oh that's right." He slapped his forehead dramatically. "You *can't* walk, can you? And you never will, you fucking crippled *cunt*!"

"Seriously?" Enhart said. "He actually called you that?"

Gloria nodded.

"I woulda kicked his ass."

She smirked. "I thought you were a pacifist."

"Listen, there are times when exceptions should be made, and that's one of them. After all he did to you, to call you *that*."

She gave him a thoughtful look, then continued. "Right. Well, I was so devastated I couldn't even reply before he turned back to the room and slammed the door behind himself. No Alphonse waiting out front this time, either. I had to call a cab, and I cried the whole way home. The house was empty, so I cracked open Bill's good bottle of scotch and started pounding it out by the pool. I hadn't been out there since I started going to Nathan's house because I didn't want Bill or Tracy to see my new wounds. Then I sat there getting hammered, staring down at the water like that day I dared myself to dive in. And the drunker I got, the more I wondered what I had to lose." She shrugged. "I'd never walk again, I knew that for sure. All my friends were dead. Nobody wanted me anymore, not even Eloise. What good was I to anybody? So I set the brakes, and I just... leaned forward until I fell face-first into the water."

Enhart nodded, thinking he knew where her story had been leading. "And you swam?"

"No, Michael. I probably could've if I wanted to. But what I wanted was to *drown*. I wished I'd died in the accident with all of my friends. So I just sank straight to the bottom and held my breath for as long as I could. By the time my body started involuntarily fighting back I couldn't get back to the surface anyway, and I *did* drown."

"Yet here you are," Enhart said.

"Here I am. Fortunately, Bill came home from work while I was out there. He happened to look out the kitchen window and saw my empty chair out by the pool, so he dove in and saved me. Once he got me breathing again he laid me down on one of the loungers and looked over all my fresh welts and scars. He looked me straight in the eye and said, 'Who did this to you, Savvy?' That's what he used to call me. And he was *furious*. '*Who did this to you?*'"

"Did you tell him?"

"If I told him, he would've killed Nathan, and as much as I wanted Nathan dead right then, I didn't want Bill to have to go to jail for murdering a billionaire. I told him they must've happened when I was on the bottom of the pool. It was obvious he didn't believe me. He'd have to be stupid not to suspect it. I'd been wearing leggings in the summer in California, and he was anything but stupid. But he nodded and said we'd figure this out together 'as a family.' But I didn't want to figure anything out. I wished he'd let me drown. My body fought against it but I still wanted to die. The week after that, they were pumping a bottle of aspirin out of my stomach at the hospital. I had to do two weeks of suicide counseling. And that's where I met Mary."

"Mary?" Enhart asked.

"Another Child of Dinah. She brought me to Mother Amelia, and Mother Amelia promised she'd give me my life back, she'd make me want to live again. She told me I might even walk again, if I wanted it badly enough."

"And you believed her."

"I was skeptical, but everyone there just looked so *blissful*. And they all said the same thing to me, or variations of it: Mother Amelia had helped them rise above their traumas. Slay their pasts and conquer their demons. By the time they told me *how*, I was already in too deep to say no, even if I'd wanted to."

Here it is, at last, Enhart thought: *the truth about what the Children of Dinah does behind closed doors.* "What'd they want you to do, Gloria?" he asked, leaning forward.

She gave him a pointed look, and said, "Kill Nathan Rowan, of course."

MIRACLES

D id you ever hear the story about the baby doll
that bled?" Gloria asked.

"Wait, back it up just a second. You just said the
Children of Dinah wanted you to *kill* your hot billionaire ex-boyfriend, and now I'm supposed to care
about some doll?"

"I'm getting there, Micheal. This is important to
the story."

He crossed his arms over his chest. "Well, bled, like
how?"

"There was this doll from the '90s," she said. "Real
Baby, it's called. I had one when I was little. You could
feed it and it moved its lips like it was chewing and
slurped up the fake mush, then a few minutes later it
would poop it out into the diaper."

"That sounds disgusting," Enhart said, thinking
about how unprepared he'd been—and still was—for
his own real baby. How long had it been since
Christie-Ann texted? Half an hour? Just twenty minutes? How long did a surgery like this take? He ought
to check in. He glanced at his phone.

"It peed too," Gloria said, and he almost had to ask

her *What did?* Then he remembered, *The random baby doll.* "You'd have to change the diapers just like a real baby."

"Hence the name, I guess."

"Right. Well, this specific doll didn't poop or pee at all. It ate the food but what came out of it wasn't brown or yellow, it was red."

"Blood?"

"Exactly. It didn't come out in the diaper, either. It bled from the palms of its hands."

"Stigmata?" Enhart asked, intrigued but skeptical.

"That's right. The kid, this poor, confused little girl, she showed the doll to her parents. They told her they'd return him—the doll—that he was defective, but the little girl begged them not to. She already loved the doll. She'd even given him a name: she called him Joshua. She cried. They felt pretty bad about trying to get rid of her doll so soon after she lost Bandit, the tabby cat they'd bought for her when she was a baby herself. So they let her keep Joshua, but she had to promise she wouldn't feed him anymore, which of course she did right away, not wanting him to starve. They took away the spoon and the little jar of fake baby food, hid em up high where she couldn't even reach them with a chair. Still, over the next week or so they kept finding these little red spots wherever she played with him. Red spots on the sofa, red spots on the carpet, red smears on the walls. The girl promised she wasn't feeding Joshua anything. She crossed her heart and hoped to die. Her parents wrapped bandages around Joshua's hands, and they'd soak through within a day. Just little weepings of blood accumulating over time. He was bleeding whether the girl fed it or not. That's when they decided something needed to be done."

"They threw the damn thing away?"

Gloria shook her head, holding his gaze. "They called their housekeeper's priest. In three days, they were told to expect a visit from the archbishop."

"They wanted to prove it was a miracle."

Again, the head shake. "They wanted to *disprove* it. Because proving it would mean they'd have to explain why a kid's toy was bleeding with the same wounds as Christ. This wasn't a statue of the Madonna weeping blood in some ancient European church. It was a little rubber baby that pisses and shits to indoctrinate little girls into wanting to be mommies."

Enhart smirked. "Isn't that what the Church wants? Be fruitful and multiply?"

"Sure. But think of how ridiculous it would've looked in the headlines. 'Vatican authenticates baby doll stigmata miracle.' Might as well say the face in that tortilla back in the '70s was a true representation of Jesus. The church doesn't even call the Shroud of Turin a true miracle. I guess they would've called it the Shroud of Taco," she said with a grin. "And that statue in Italy, the Madonna that wept blood, they discovered it was the blood of a male pig."

Enhart snorted. "Probably a male *chauvinist* pig, too."

Gloria frowned. He figured she was probably too young to understand the reference, despite the phrase being somewhat associated with her namesake, Gloria Steinem. "Anyway, the archbishop and his team arrived to investigate. They were only there for a very short time. They spoke with the girl and her parents and the housekeeper, then they left—promising they would be back soon with Joshua, who they needed to run tests on, and their decision."

"Was it a miracle then?"

"No. A week later, they returned to the house, and told them all it was an elaborate hoax. They'd filled Joshua with liquid and found indents and tiny holes where the liquid came out, which they determined with a hypodermic syringe. And the blood they tested was feline blood. A cat's. They couldn't test Bandit's blood because he was buried in the yard, but since the vet determined he'd died of acute anemia, it didn't take a genius to figure out what happened."

"Blood loss," Enhart said.

"Right. It turned out their deeply religious house-keeper had been taking blood from the cat and injecting it into the palms of the doll so they'd weep like Christ's wounds. She confessed to the whole thing the moment the archbishop revealed their findings, got down on her knees weeping and begging him to forgive her."

"Mystery solved then," Enhart said.

"Mystery solved," Gloria agreed. "Sometimes miracles only *seem* like miracles, until you take the time to scratch beneath the surface."

"Okay." He uncrossed his arms. "So what are you telling me here?"

"You know the story of Simon Magus, from the bible? Simon the Sorcerer?"

"Sure. He was a Samaritan. 'The Bad Samaritan' he's called sometimes. An illusionist in the time of Jesus. The, uh... the David Copperfield of his time."

"From the Dickens book?"

Enhart frowned. "No, the magician. Made the Statue of Liberty disappear?" Gloria didn't clue in so he tried the only other thing he remembered about the guy. "Used to be married to Claudia Schiffer?"

"Oh *him*," she said. "Right. Like David Copperfield then. Or more like David Blaine, with the levitation. Back then I guess it was easier to trick people into thinking illusions were miracles, and there were a lot more people vying to be the next Messiah. Simon Magus was baptized by Phillip the Evangelist. In the *Acts of Peter*, he was seen levitating and flying over his audience in the Roman Forum to prove he was a god, and Peter the Apostle prayed for God to stop him from flying. It doesn't say whether or not he was *literally* flying by some supernatural means or if it was some kind of high-wire act—"

"Be tough to cover up the kind of scaffolding you'd need for a trick like that in an open-roof venue," Enhart said.

"Right. Whatever it was, whether God took away his power or the rope snapped, abracadabra! Simon fell and broke his legs in three places. He's supposed to have died in surgery."

Enhart's heart seized. He looked at the phone. No messages.

"*Are* you okay, Michael?"

He turned back to her, swallowing hard. "I'm fine. You were saying..."

"You know about the Simonians? That Gnostic cult based around Simon Magus?"

Enhart shook his head. "Not really."

"Well in the first and second centuries, there was a Hebrew sect of Gnostics called the Simonians. According to their doctrine, the world was created by angels, not by God. And Eden wasn't an actual garden. It's actually a metaphor for the womb. Umbilical cords are the river out of Eden."

"Weird," Enhart said. "But what's that all got to do with miracles?"

Gloria smiled patiently. "You don't have to lead all

the time, Michael. Just follow along. For once in your life."

Enhart glanced at the painting and almost crossed his arms again. He picked absently under his fingernails instead. "Lead away," he said.

"What I'm saying is, if the womb is the Garden of Eden, then it stands to reason our mothers are God, expelling us from the garden into the harsh realities of the world."

"Interesting theory," he said.

"You said your mother died a long time ago. What do you remember about her?"

Enhart smiled. He saw no harm telling her about his mother. It wasn't like she could use her against him, seeing as she'd been dead for over forty years. "She had the most beautiful voice," he said. He couldn't picture her face, it had been so long since he'd seen her. But her voice he remembered with perfect clarity. "She used to sing... while she worked, when she relaxed, just about all the time. And there was so much *joy* in it. Listening to her sing made everyone around her happy."

Gloria smiled. "That's nice. Is that all you remember?"

"I remember her smell. Like wild roses." He considered it a moment. He hadn't thought about her, *truly* reminisced, in such a long time doing so now made his heart physically hurt. "She had this tattoo. On her shoulder," he said, pointing to his own left shoulder. "A pair of red lips. Only it was bumpy, like real lips. I used to kiss it sometimes when I was really little, just to make her laugh. Her laugh was musical too. The kind that makes *you* laugh, you know?"

Gloria nodded. "I know what you mean. I'm sorry you lost her. She sounds like a good mother."

"Your mother's a good woman too," Enhart said. "She may not be perfect, you obviously have your differences, but she cared enough about you to hire me to bring you back."

Gloria shrugged. "Maybe. And maybe someday I'll try to reconcile with that."

"I hope you can," Enhart said genuinely.

She smiled. Then she turned toward the bedside table, where his cell phone lay beside the clock radio. "Can we listen to the radio? Just for a minute?"

"Are the Children of Dinah not allowed to listen to music?"

She frowned, then laughed off the comment. "Of course. We have CDs and all that. I just haven't listened to the radio since... God, I can't remember when. Sometimes it's just nice to let fate pick the songs for you, you know?"

Enhart chuckled. "Yeah, I guess I do." He sat up and turned it on.

"*Heaven, I'm in heaven,*" Fred Astaire crooned. His father used to play this song on the old cassette player in the rust-speckled 1981 Datsun 210 station wagon they drove around in from town to town, motel to motel, all across America. Of all the musical eras and genres Fate could have chosen for them, this was one of the worst.

"Someone left it on the A.M.," he said, quickly reaching to change it.

"Leave it."

He paused with his fingers hovering over the switch. He didn't like listening to these moldy oldies. They reminded him too much of those road trips, learning "the ropes" from his old man. All those sad people. The crying, screaming and fighting.

He'd been too young to fully understand what his

father did then, and by the time he did understand he was already working alongside him, following in his footsteps, rescuing the victims of false prophets and phony messiahs, and bringing them back to freedom, whether they wanted it or not.

It was a noble cause, he'd eventually been able to admit. But parts of the process, at least under his father's tutelage, had always been repugnant to him, and not just because of the violence he'd experienced firsthand from the old man. These people were *happy* when his father rescued them from their communities, at least in their own minds. It was Stockholm Syndrome, obviously. They weren't able to distinguish between real happiness and the *forced* happiness caused by constant love bombing and other intense group dynamics.

In his father's world, this brainwashing needed to be countered by its opposites. Love could only be conquered by violence. Devotion by hate.

Since the year Enhart turned thirteen, he'd told himself he'd never be anything like his father. It was why he chose listening and understanding over threats of violence. Why he chose love and forgiveness over hate and wrath. It was a hard path to follow sometimes, but a righteous one.

Gloria was leaning back against the headboard, smiling as she listened to the song. It was a sad smile, like those worn by the various cult victims he and his father had liberated over the years, once they'd finally been set free. A tear formed at the corner of her right eye and spilled down her cheek.

Enhart figured he knew what she was thinking. A song about dancing, when she'd never be able to dance again. It was pretty basic math, and he almost considered asking her to dance himself just to cheer her up. He could let her rest her feet on his shoes and carry her around the room. But he had two left feet. He was as much a slave to his ungainly body as she was to her broken one.

Even if I can't follow the beat, I'd rather lead, he thought, remembering what she'd said about him before the song. He'd inherited that hard-headedness from his father too.

When the song ended, an overly animated DJ barged in. Enhart couldn't help but imagine him as the Kool-Aid Man. *"You're listening to WBBL, the Bull, Buffalo's only golden oldies station. That was 'Cheek to Cheek' by Fred Astaire, from the—"*

Enhart flicked off the radio and sat again.

Gloria wiped away her tears and looked at him, still wearing that sad smile. "Is it better to be free and miserable or enslaved and happy?" she asked him after a long moment of silence.

"Are you asking me that, or is it rhetorical?"

"I'm asking you."

"It's better to be free than a slave," he said matter-of-factly.

"Do you really believe that, Michael, or are you just saying it because it's what you're *supposed* to believe?"

Then he did cross his arms. "I'm not gonna debate slavery with you here, Gloria."

"Fine, I'll put it another way. Is it better to lead or follow? I'm guessing I already know your answer."

He smirked. "That depends."

"On what?"

"On who the leader is."

"So you *would* follow someone, if that someone knows what they're doing."

"And they're on the right side, morally."

Gloria nodded thoughtfully. "But morals are subjective."

"Some aren't."

"Like what?"

"Rape. Murder."

"But murder is okay in war. You said that earlier."

"That depends on the *method* of murder. That's why we have the Geneva Convention."

"Okay. So short of torture, gassing, things like that —the cruel and unusual stuff—you're okay with murder if it's for the greater good."

"Sure, of course."

"Then why are you so adamantly against revenge? There are *thousands* of serial rapists out there right now. If you could kill them all with a single press of a button and spare thousands more victims, wouldn't you do it?"

"No."

She blinked at him, skeptical. "Why not?"

"Because of the Butterfly Effect, I guess. You can't know how many peoples' lives are made better with those rapists in it, can you? They might have wives, children, *grand*children. Isn't it better to rehabilitate them instead?"

"Well, what about murderers? What if someone killed your baby girl? Wouldn't you want that man dead?"

Enhart had a kneejerk visceral reaction to the question, his guts twisting in knots at the thought of the surgeon cutting her open, nicking an artery, unable to stop the bleeding. Then her heart giving out, the machine flatlining. He had to prevent himself from moaning.

"That's different," he said finally, swallowing hard.

"Why is it different?"

"Because," he said, and couldn't finish the thought.

"Because then it's no longer a thought experiment," she finished for him.

"Okay," he said, neither agreeing nor disagreeing. "I see your point. But Nathan Rowan didn't *kill anyone*, did he? And he didn't..." He lowered his voice, as he'd just about been yelling. "...*rape* you, either—at least you didn't mention anything about that. If he did, that's a different story."

"No. He didn't rape me, Michael." She gave him a plain look. "And if you want to get technical, *I* assaulted *him*."

Enhart shrugged. Judging by her story it'd been pretty plain the guy had *wanted* to consummate their strange relationship, but for some reason couldn't allow himself to. Some deep-seated psychological thing probably rooted in the art piece he never should've been allowed to witness in the first place.

Maybe Nathan Rowan should've murdered the performance artist, Enhart thought amusedly. *Guy sounds like a real piece of work.*

"We're all slaves to what other people decided is *good* or *righteous* or *morally acceptable* two thousand fucking years ago. But you admitted it yourself, morality is subjective in some cases. Like power, the truth is malleable. That's what I learned from the Mother Amelia and the Children of Dinah. They taught me that to control my own destiny, I had to let go of certain notions about reality. And one of those things was that murder is *inherently evil*."

Enhart merely shook his head.

"Mary," Gloria said, "the woman I met in the hospital—"

—SHE TOLD me that story about the baby doll. It was her doll. That was the wound Mother Amelia helped her heal, even though it was a trauma later in life that set her on the path toward the Children of Dinah.

For me, it turned out it wasn't my Little Act of God. That's what put me on the path, but Nathan's betrayal was my core trauma. If I'd never met Nathan, things would've gone in an entirely different direction. I could've gone on to have a perfectly normal, unfulfilling life, like all the rest of you sheep. Mother Amelia helped me to understand that Nathan offering to help me walk again and *snatching* away that hope actually *freed* me. Without that betrayal, I might never have found her Light in the darkness.

But to truly understand that, I had to kill him first.

When he woke up in the barn and saw us standing around him, our shadows circling him just outside of the light shining down on his face, he was so calm. He thought he could just pay us all off, could *buy* us. Everything in his life up to that moment, he'd solved with money. He couldn't possibly fathom someone who couldn't be bought, and even when it was clear we wanted something other than money, he was still counting on one of us to break.

Then I wheeled out of the circle, into the light.

"So that's what this is," he said with a smug grin. "The little crippled cunt finally decided to fight back. Did this little whore tell you all what she did? Why I broke it off with her?" When nobody responded, he told them his version of the story, which was pretty much the same as mine, only he left out the part where he whipped me to orgasm day after day and said instead that he was "helping me recover from my trauma." That we were getting over it together.

When it finally dawned on him all of his money and fancy words couldn't buy him out of his fate, he changed tactics.

"Look at you, Savannah," he said. "You look so different. You know why I wanted you? Because you were broken, yeah, but because you were *malleable*. Like fresh clay. I knew with some tough love, with the right discipline, I could mold you into someone truly capable of anything. Isn't that what you wanted? Now here you are: strong, beautiful. Defiant. You really are perfect, Savannah."

I listened to all his honey-coated bullshit, then I said, "My name is *Gloria*," the name I'd chosen, for the time when I finally rose above my past, which was right then.

And I slashed his throat.

Unless you've experienced it yourself, you can't possibly imagine the *transformative power* of revenge. *True* revenge. I was baptized in his blood. It washed over me like a wave of pure bliss. If I could've stood up right then I would've danced in it like a hippy at some jam band concert. I let it pour down my throat and it *quenched* me like a desert oasis. It tasted *sweet*.

"Now walk," Mother Amelia said.

I looked around at the others, who'd all stepped into the light with me. She had to be joking. I wasn't sure yet. I didn't fully *believe*.

"*Walk*, Gloria," she said, calling me by my new name, now that I'd been baptized in the blood of my enemy.

"*Walk*," the other Children chanted. "*Walk, walk, walk...*"

I gripped the arms of my chair. I lifted my right

foot down so it lay flat on the dirt floor of the barn, then my left, and with all of my strength I pushed myself to stand. My legs shook, just like that first day I'd hung from the shackles in Nathan Rowan's atelier, but I stood. I *stood*, Michael. And while the Children chanted around me, I walked, like a newborn fawn, to Nathan Rowan's corpse. I felt like I was towering over him, this person who'd held me back, who'd made me so weak I tried to take my own life not once but twice, now he was just a shell, an empty vessel. A *nothing*.

I stood over him and said, "Thank you." I looked at the others, my brothers and sisters, and thanked them. Then Mother Amelia came over, and told me how proud she was of me.

And then we burned him like we did to all the others.

"WAIT A MINUTE," Enhart interrupted. "You said this was what—2012? 2013?"

Gloria gave him a quizzical look. "It was December, 2013 by the time we got to this stage in my enlightenment."

"Okay, so how come I never heard about this? When that Luigi guy shot that billionaire it was all over the news, twenty-four-seven. How come I never heard about this Nathan Rowan guy getting whacked?"

"Whacked?" Gloria said, smirking.

Enhart noticed the double entendre and snorted a laugh. "I'm serious. How come I never heard about it?"

"I don't know, Michael. His disappearance was all

over local L.A. news for at least a month before they called off the search."

Enhart hummed thoughtfully, then looked down at her legs. She said she'd walked, but now she needed her chair. He'd seen her rolling around the compound in it while he'd done his recon over the past several days. She hadn't even been able to get to the bathroom by herself. Obviously being able to get up out of her wheelchair by the healing power of vengeance was horseshit. And this was supposed to be one of the "three miracles" she'd promised?

"I guess your miracle didn't last all that long, huh?"

She looked at him plainly. "What do you mean?"

He nodded at her legs. "You can't walk anymore. Can't even stand. What did Mother Amelia have to say when you fell back down on your ass?"

Gloria smiled—almost smugly, Enhart thought— and peered down at her own legs. He followed her gaze, startling as her right big toe began to wiggle. She followed this by clenching both feet, one after the other.

"Abracadabra," she said.

He caught her eye again as it dawned on him.

The bitch can walk!

Before he could react, Gloria leaped out of bed and bolted for the door. She'd already pulled the latch by the time Enhart rounded the foot of the bed. She turned the deadbolt and had the door yanked open an inch when he reached her and slammed his palm against it.

Gloria spun on the balls of her feet to face him, swinging out simultaneously to slap him. He caught her by the wrist and held it against the door, grabbed her other arm and pinned her there, her toes—her very clearly able-bodied toes—barely touching the floor.

"*Let me go!*" she yelled up at him, struggling to free herself from his grip.

"*Stop fighting!*" he roared down at her, pinning her legs to the door with a knee.

Squirming under his weight and pressing her boobs against his chest, she moved a hip seductively into his groin, her big eyes moist with tears and her lips parted.

Enhart held her, looking down at her, realizing she wasn't trying to get away anymore, she was trying to seduce him. He wouldn't let her. He loved his wife. His dick might be a traitor, getting hard despite himself, but he didn't cheat. *Not once*. And anyway, this was just another of her head games. He'd been stupid to let her out of the handcuffs so early. Stupid to carry her to the bathroom. Stupid to tell her anything about Christie-Ann and Jessa and himself. He'd trusted her and played right into her goddamn hands.

"Kiss me, Michael," she said, her breath prickling the hairs on the back of his neck.

"No," he said. Weakly, if he had to be honest.

Despite his lack of consent, Gloria craned her neck and kissed him, open mouth, her warm, wet tongue spiraling around his.

Enhart didn't realize just how badly he'd wanted her until a moan escaped him and he kissed her back, thrusting himself against her small body, pressing her against the door. Her legs squirmed against him, no longer fighting, rubbing herself against his now-throbbing hard-on.

A buzz startled him.

He pulled his lips away from hers but she looked

at him with what seemed like fury and pressed her lips back into his, just about eating his face.

The phone buzzed again.

Not a text. A call.

He let her go. Gloria dropped to her feet, panting. Then she slapped him across the face. Hard enough to sting.

Before she could hit him again, Enhart grabbed her around the waist and threw her over his shoulder, the way he had when he'd brought her to and from his car. Punches hammered down on his back as he fireman-carried her back to the bed.

He tossed her down on the mattress. She tried to scurry away on her hands and knees but he grabbed her by the collar of her hemp pajamas and dragged her back. She threw another punch. He deflected it and grabbed her wrist, wrenched it back to the headboard and latched her to it as she clawed at him with her free hand.

Her nails, short and blunt, still managed to do damaged to his neck. He'd have a lot of explaining to do when he got done with this job.

"Let me go, you mother—" she started. Enhart had already snatched the duct tape from his duffel bag and tore off a strip. He slapped it over her lips in mid-protest.

While she shouted under the tape, he grabbed the phone off the bedside table. Five rings. Christie-Ann would be getting worried, but she knew he was in the middle of a job. She wouldn't suspect anything. And really, what had he done? Momentarily reciprocated when another woman literally threw herself at him? Could he be faulted for that?

Gloria's screams were muffled by the tape. She jerked desperately on the cuffs, rattling the headboard.

"You'll keep quiet if you know what's good for you," he warned her, reminding himself unpleasantly of his father. What would he do if she didn't? Beat her? He wasn't that man. He'd *never be* that man.

He opened the door, stepped out quickly to the sound of her muffled screams, and slammed it behind himself.

"Fucking psycho," he muttered, then picked up the phone. "Sorry," he said. "I was in the middle of something. How is she?"

Christie-Ann spoke. Her voice sounded much better than last time. Cheerier. And with the news she gave him, he could understand why.

The surgery went well, as good as could be expected. The surgeon said it'll be a tough road ahead but he expected Jessa would recover swiftly and be as good as new in no time at all.

"*It's a miracle*," Christie-Ann said.

Enhart glanced at the door to room 9.

"It is," he said, though he still didn't believe in them. He *couldn't* believe in them. "I love you, Bunches."

"I love you, Cinnamon Roll."

He flushed hearing her pet name for him as a woman came out of a room three down from his, though he knew the woman wouldn't have heard it. He hated when people had conversations on speakerphone in public, and always kept his earpiece on the lowest possible volume that he could still hear.

She was a bigger woman, wearing a red shawl draped over her shoulders and a gold lamé minidress over a pair of tights, whose pattern he couldn't make out from the distance. Christie-Ann might have called her "hefty," though she seemed to carry her weight well, sashaying away from the door and sucking on an e-cigarette. She caught his eye as she turned to exhale.

"Oh, hi," she said, twiddling the fingers of her right hand. Her voice was soft and somewhat sultry. If she was a hundred pounds lighter, she might've been considered conventionally attractive. Her smile was undoubtably pretty. "Are you with the convention?" she asked.

"Convention?" The guy at the desk had told him the motel was empty aside from one room.

"You didn't see? Big busload of people came in before dark, dropped off—mmm, must've been twenty, thirty people. I figured it was probably a tour, even though it was an old school bus, but I was told it was a convention."

Enhart frowned, looking up and down at the rows of closed doors and windows with shut blinds. His car was still the only one in the lot. "What sort of convention?"

"Melvin didn't say." She took a pull on her vape and ginned.

"Is Melvin that reject from the Sunshine Band at the front desk?"

The woman snorted a laugh. "That's him. He's quite the character once you get to know him. I'm hoping it's something fun like furries. We don't get many conventions here at the Lonely, even though you could spit and hit the airport. Not that kind of place."

Enhart hummed thoughtfully. *How long do I have to stand here and make small talk so I don't look like I've got something to hide?* he wondered. Then he thought: *Did she hear Gloria screaming? Is she feeling me out right now?*

"I'm Mike," he said, anxious to get back to the

room, but aware he'd already made himself memorable by not lying and telling her he was with whatever this convention was.

"Shyla," she said, twiddling her fingers again.

"Nice to meet you. "

"Likewise. You here on business yourself?"

"Yes, ma'am."

She laughed again. "'Ma'am.' Well, I don't wanna keep you."

"Thanks," he said, nodding dumbly.

She turned back toward the door to her room, blowing out a cloud of vape smoke.

"Flowers," he called out abruptly. He wasn't sure why he'd said it, but now that he had, he couldn't take it back.

She turned back. "Excuse me?"

"I sell flowers," he said. "I'm a wholesaler."

"Oh?" She raised a thinly plucked eyebrow, making him think of Nathan Rowan's secretary-slash-mother, if either person even existed.

"Yup," he said. "Most of my job is driving from store to store. Nothing too exciting."

"Nurseries," she said.

"Huh?" he asked, wondering what it had to do with children.

"Where they sell flowers."

"Right. Nurseries," he said. "Lotta department stores, too."

She smiled. "I love flowers. Tulips are my favorite. White tulips."

"Yeah. They're good ones, all right."

She smiled again. "Well, you have yourself a good night, flower man."

"You too..." He struggled to remember her name.

"Shyla," she reminded him.

"You too, Shyla."

"You really should consider those tulips," she said.

He gave her a questioning look.

"For your business partner."

Had she seen him come in with Gloria? Had she *heard* her?

"Oh, right," he said. "Why tulips?"

"Well, I didn't mean to eavesdrop, but it sounded like you two were having a bit of a tiff before you stepped out here."

"Oh. Sorry about that. Bit of a difference of opinion. About the fall line," he added, and winced inwardly.

"I guess even pretty things can be ugly business."

He chuckled. "Why white tulips, by the way?"

"They're a symbol of forgiveness. When a man buys me white tulips, I just *melt*."

His spine went cold. What were the odds of her using the exact word Gloria had used to describe her reaction to Nathan Rowan begging her to be his bondage slave? How many women actually *melted*?

He shook off the unease. She couldn't have heard. Even if Boney M. in the front office had fibbed about the soundproofing, Gloria had been speaking at a normal volume when she'd said it. It wasn't possible for Sheila to have heard that part of the story from three doors down. Not without the sort of audio equipment he used in his reconnaissance. Not unless the room was bugged.

Don't be paranoid. Nobody's watching. Nobody's listening in. It's just a coincidence, that's all.

"I'll consider it, thanks," he said. "You have a good night."

"You too."

She returned to her room, leaving him standing alone in the crisp autumn air.

White tulips, he thought, huffing a laugh. He remembered what Gloria had said about Sister Amelia and her assaulters: "This isn't a story about forgiveness, Michael. It's about *wrath*."

I've gotta turn this around somehow, he thought. *There's still time. I fucked up, but I don't think it's FUBAR just yet. I can still bring her around. I know I can do it.*

Looking up and down the length of the motel again, the sense of unease returned. A school bus? Who rents a school bus for a convention?

The blinds in the room to the right of Shyla's shook against the glass.

Was someone watching him?

Forget it, Mike. You're not doing anything wrong. Her mother hired *you to get her poor crippled kid out of a* murder *cult, for Christ's sake. Okay, the money's good, but the Children of Dinah don't exactly have a good reputation, and it turns out it's worse than they thought, if any of what Gloria said is true. Local PD'd probably* commend *me for this.*

With a resolute nod, he gave a Boy Scout salute to the window where the blinds had moved, then headed back to the room, prepared to take this to the next level.

Gloria may have gotten him to violate the two most crucial of his hard-and-fast rules—no violence, no sexual contact—but he wouldn't allow her to push him any further.

It was his turn to be the leader.

GUILT

G loria gave him a baleful look when he returned to the room. "I'm thirsty," she said, once he'd peeled the tape off her lips.

"I already got you a pop."

"I could use some water. My throat's really dry."

"I dunno, your tongue felt pretty moist shoved halfway down my throat."

She chuckled bitterly. "Come on, Michael. Just a little sip."

"Sorry." He shrugged. "You lost your privileges when you tried to escape."

Gloria tsked. "I wasn't really gonna do it. I was just messing around."

"Fuck around, find out. Isn't that what the kids say?"

"I'm almost thirty, Michael. How would I know what the kids say? Or would you prefer it if I was a kid?"

He leaned back against the closet door and crossed his arms, not about to dignify her baiting with a response.

"Don't be like that." She pouted. "You wanted it too."

"Say that same thing to Nathan, did you?"

She pursed her lips.

"You and I, we need to come to a little under-standing," he said. "No bathroom privileges, no water, no food. Not until you start telling me *the truth*."

"I never lied to you, Michael."

"Yeah? I'm sure you really wanted to kiss me just then too, huh?"

She shrugged the shoulder of her cuffed hand. "I dunno. You just seem so sad. I wanted to make you happy."

"Quit fucking with me, *Savannah*."

Gloria scowled. "*Stop it*."

"Why? That's your name, isn't it? You said it your-self, multiple times."

"That's who I *was*, not who I *am*."

"Right. Savannah was a poor little crippled girl, taken advantage of by some spoiled rich player. *Gloria* can walk. *Gloria* doesn't take shit from anyone. Gloria 'slays her demons,' doesn't she?"

She raised her chin defiantly.

"But Gloria's also been brainwashed by a murder cult," he said.

Her chin dropped, and she scowled up at him. "It's not a *murder* cult."

"You just admitted there's the ashes of at least one body on the compound, and implied there's more. Tell me how that's not the *definition* of a murder cult."

"It's not like we're killing random people, Michael."

"What difference does that make? You think *mo-tive* is gonna sway a jury? Maybe in your Mother

Amelia's case they'd give her a little leeway, because of the abuse she suffered when she was a kid, statute of limitations." He scoffed. "What you did? That's premeditated, lady. First-degree murder. You're looking at life in prison, that's if you're lucky."

Gloria smirked. "You can't take away what the Children of Dinah gave me. Mother Amelia's love made me stronger than you can ever imagine."

"Hell, she helped you walk again." He threw up his hands like a Southern Baptist, shouting, "*Hallelujah!*" Then, softer: "Only, let's just say I don't believe it."

She raised her right leg, running her toes up and down the calf of the left seductively, holding his gaze. "The proof's right here."

"Spontaneous regeneration."

"That's a miracle in itself, isn't it?"

"I don't know, Gloria. Maybe you lied about not seeing Rowan's spinal surgeon. Maybe you had the surgery after all, and it worked. You were an actor in school, right? Or hell, for all I know, you were faking it the whole time."

She shook her head derisively. "What will it take for you to *believe*?"

"You promised me *three* miracles, in case you forgot. Right now, all I have is the word of some little dick tease actor-slash-model-slash-murderer. Why should I believe a goddamn word you say?"

She laughed again, brightly, like he hadn't just insulted her. They studied each other in silence, quietly judging one another. "How many people have you converted so far?" she said finally.

"This isn't about me."

"How many? You remember that, don't you?"

"Thirty-five," he said, though he couldn't be confident in the answer.

"*Forty-two*, Michael. And two of them were my friends."

"How would you know that?"

"And what do you get out of it? Other than money?"

"I asked how you know that."

"You researched us, Michael. *We* researched *you*. After you took Sonny and Cher—"

This time Enhart smirked. "How did that work, by the way? I figured they must've been a couple when they joined, but neither of them told me much at all. They were so eager to get out, they didn't even put up a fight. Explain that if your Mother Amelia is so wise and powerful."

"You're right, they were a couple. Without Sonny, Cher was weaker than the rest of us. Once you took her, it broke him. His father was counting on that. What he wasn't counting on was what Sonny did a few weeks after you pulled him out." She let the comment hang a moment. "How do you feel about that, by the way?"

Enhart crossed his arms over his chest again. "What do you mean?" he asked, knowing exactly what she meant.

"I guess you must've heard Sonny committed suicide."

He winced. Sonny, aka Trudy Beaumont, had been a star college athlete when he met Cher, aka Lucy Trillio. Then Trudy dropped out of school to follow her on what his father, Tobias, had called "some b.s. hippie vision quest." Enhart hadn't known Tobias Beaumont's true connection to Cher when he'd pulled her out of the Children of Dinah. Tobias had claimed she was his goddaughter. Once Enhart made the connection, it was already too late. Both Trudy and Lucy were free.

Except they'd never gotten back together. Lucy had vanished without a trace and Trudy committed suicide shortly after. The kid had still had a bright future ahead of him. Despite dropping out, the way he'd played, any college would've been jumping over themselves to sign him. And Tobias Beaumont was wealthy enough to pay a hundred grand for Enhart to deprogram each kid. He could only assume Trudy had been so devastated by the loss of Lucy he couldn't bear to live any more.

Real star-crossed lovers stuff.

When Enhart found out about it, about Trudy's suicide, he'd been devastated himself. He'd thought a lot about what his father had done to him, how he'd felt in the following months and years, and the worst of it was, he *understood* Trudy's decision to take his own life. He'd felt that same desperation, that same loss, as acutely as a missing limb.

The day he'd lost his mother had been the last truly happy day of his life, at least until he met Christie-Ann, and the day their precious little Jessa came into the world. The two of them had filled the hole his father had torn in his heart that night so many years ago.

But he couldn't let his visceral reaction to Sonny's suicide show on his face now, despite the immense guilt he felt for pulling the kid out of the Children of Dinah. Gloria was baiting him. He figured they must've started looking into him and Bob Ingles shortly after he'd pulled out Sonny and Cher. He'd kidnapped and converted two of Mother Amelia's

Children. It was only natural they'd want some sort of revenge.

If anyone took my little girl....

He supposed he was just lucky they hadn't decided to do what Sister Amelia had to the priest and the exorcist, and what Gloria had done to the billionaire bad boy.

"I heard," he said finally. "It was a senseless tragedy. I felt for his family's loss."

"Thoughts and prayers," Gloria said dismissively. "That call you just got. That was your wife, wasn't it? That's why you freaked."

He looked at her accusingly. "You don't know anything about me."

"I know a lot more about you than you think. I know you've been doing this so long you probably don't even remember a time when you weren't. I know your mother died, a long time ago. I know you're married. Happily, for the most part. I know you have a little girl who's fighting for her life in an incubator right now, born premature. And I know that if you accept Mother Amelia's gift, that struggle will be over before you know it. She can perform *miracles,* if you accept her love. Why won't you accept her love, Michael?"

Jessa could've died in that operating room, he thought, *but she survived. Christie-Ann said it herself: it was a miracle. Why is it so hard for you to* believe?

"Because I don't believe you," he said. "And you know what? I don't think you believe it either. You've been selling yourself this bull for so long it feels like gospel." The word *bull* made him glance at the painting of the father and son, and the ominous feeling returned. "But what was it you said? Scratch a miracle, find a lie?"

"You twisted my words."

"That's right. You said, 'some miracles only seem like it until you scratch under the surface.' What'd you mean by that, if you honestly believe what happened to you was miraculous?"

Gloria closed her mouth. Said nothing.

"Exactly. I caught you in a lie, Gloria. Hell, maybe every damn thing you've said to me was lies. And why not? Once an actor, always an actor, right? And you said yourself the Children of Dinah were researching me. You probably know how many victims of sick cults like yours I've brought back more than I do myself."

"Forty-two," Gloria said again. "Forty-two people whose hearts you've stripped the Light from. Forty-two people you've taken from their rightful families, from the people who accepted them and loved them when their biological families wouldn't. Forty-two people who were living happily, free from the shackles of this capitalist pigsty nightmare, you threw them right back into that open sewer of a world out there," she said, nodding toward the door. "Are you proud of yourself?"

Enhart bristled. "Of course I'm proud. Why wouldn't I be? You're looking at it the wrong way, Gloria. Yeah, the world out there can be pretty shitty. Sure, it's tough, especially when you feel like you got no love out there to rely on. But you've *got* that love, Gloria. Bill and Tracy, however you feel about them, they paid me to help you. That's why you're here. Because they loved you enough to call me. Think of it like an intervention. You're *addicted* to the Children of Dinah. Your parents just want to help get you *clean*."

"You're not gonna guilt-trip me into giving up my family."

Gloria's words triggered a memory, and he thought he might be able to use what she'd said as ammunition against her spiritual leader. "Speaking of giving up family," he said, "whatever happened to Mother Amelia's baby? The one the nuns got adopted. If she's so big on family, why'd she let her own kid go without their mother?"

"She found her son and embraced him into her heart."

"*Kidnapped* him, you mean. From his adoptive parents."

"Liberated him from false imprisonment."

"Kind of like what I've done to you, huh?"

"If you say so."

Enhart pushed himself off the wall and sat in the chair. He picked the pop can up off the floor and shook it, drank the dregs out of it and uttered an exaggerated sigh. "So this kid," he said, smacking his lips, "he grew up in the Children of Dinah?"

Gloria shook her head, watching the can as he returned it to the floor. She had a noticeable look of disappointment when she said, "The Children of Dinah didn't exist yet."

"How'd the other nuns react to a baby in the convent then?"

"Amelia left the church the minute she got her revenge and never went back. Not to the convent either."

"So it was just Amelia then. Her and her little boy."

"No. She met someone."

"A man?"

Gloria shook her head. "A *prophet*."

"Of course. I bet he taught her every trick in the cult leader playbook too."

"He *freed* her. Because after she slayed her demons, she felt guilty. But it was misplaced guilt. Like the guilt you feel over Sonny's suicide." She held his gaze. "No one ever found Cher, did you know that? Her parents still have no idea where she is."

Enhart nodded. He knew that, and he also knew it was very possible, even *likely*, she'd also killed herself. A true Romeo and Juliet situation.

"Do you ever check in on the people you supposedly 'liberate'?" she asked, putting air quotes around her final word.

"Yeah, I do. Most of them are doing well. Some of em aren't. Doing what I do, it's not a one-stop solution. It's a hard road back sometimes. Like coming back from addiction. Sometimes it's just substituting one addiction for another, and hoping it's not as harmful."

"And you truly believe what you're doing is good," she said. "That it's *righteous*."

"Yes, I honestly do," he said, before he could change his mind again.

"Then why are you so sad?"

He frowned. "Hate to disappoint you, Gloria, but I'm *not* sad. I love my work. I've got a beautiful wife waiting for me at home, and a healthy baby girl. What have I got to be sad about?"

Rather than reply, she turned to the door. "My friend, Mary, she belonged to the Happy Face cult before she became one of Dinah's Children."

Enhart sneered.

"You've heard of them?"

"Of course I've heard of them. Real nutjobs. They all killed themselves."

"Right. Basically they were Scientology if Scientology was a death cult. Anyway, before she joined Happy Face, Mary was a gymnast in high school."

Enhart stopped himself from saying his wife was a gymnast in high school too. It'd be just the sort of thing Gloria would try to exploit. "Is this another of your miracle stories?" he asked instead.

"No, Michael. But this story *is* important."

"All right," he said. "Mary's the same girl who had the baby doll, right? The one who pulled you into the CoD?"

"That's her. Everyone had such high hopes for her. Her mom, her coach, her school, even her hometown. Then she fractured her talus bone in two places during the Olympic Trial, landing badly on the vault."

Enhart winced. "That's tough. Any kind of sport is a fickle bitch. Just ask Bo Jackson."

Gloria frowned. "Who?"

"Never mind."

"Mary was devastated," Gloria went on. "She couldn't get over the guilt she felt for disappointing everyone. She'd been a *hometown hero*. Her going to the Olympics was gonna put that little Podunk town on the map."

"It's not fair to put that sort of pressure on a kid," Enhart said.

"Right. But they did, and so did her mother and coach. Then she goes and breaks her ankle, and suddenly all they'd been training for, for hours on end every day, all the pain, the frustration, the bills, everything they'd *sacrificed for her*, all of it was gone with the snap of a two-inch bone. They had nothing left to root for. Her coach left town. Found some other girl in some other small town to pin his hopes and dreams on. And her mother fell into a deep depression."

"What happened to her dad? When you told the story about the baby doll, she had both parents. A nanny too."

"Her dad died a few years after the Real Baby incident. Blood cancer, of all things. Her mother blamed his death on the housekeeper, and what she called her 'crazy voodoo baby doll.'"

"A few knives short of a drawer, huh?"

"Mary thought she had undiagnosed schizophrenia, which of course the Happy Cult didn't believe in. And after Mary's injury at the Olympic Trial, her mother became a menace. She made Carrie White's mom seem like Mother of the Year."

Enhart frowned. "That's the second time you mentioned her. Who's this Carrie White person?"

Gloria blinked at him. "From the movie?" she said. "Stephen King?"

"Sorry." He shrugged. "Like I said, I'm not a horror fan."

"Well, she's basically a psychotic Jesus nut who bullies her teenage daughter so badly Carrie goes Columbine on her high school prom after the other kids drench her in pig's blood. That's the gist of it, anyway."

"Oh right. I know that one."

"But Mary's mom was almost worse. Kept telling Mary she failed her, failed the whole town, that she ruined their lives, and everyone hated her for it, including all of her friends. Meanwhile Mary was still walking around on crutches."

"That's terrible. She was already suffering enough."

"Exactly. So the Happy Face people found out about her crushed Olympic dreams and sought her out. Their PR reps thought she was just the kind of person they could use as the face of their 'brand.' Like what Tom Cruise did for Xenu."

"Not quite though. Mary didn't even have a Wheaties box."

"No, but her story was pretty big in the local news for a while there, as one of those 'personal tragedy' pieces."

"Tug at the heartstrings." He shook his head. "I don't watch the news much."

"You're not a fan of horror, I know."

He grinned. "Exactly. Plus, I'm on the road a lot and most of these cheap hotels have shitty TVs and spotty cable."

"We don't have televisions in the community," Gloria said. "Mother Amelia says it 'blinds the third eye.'"

"I could see that." He considered what he'd just said and added, "No pun intended." Then he shrugged. "My dad used to say it 'rots the mind.'"

"Yeah," she said. "So the Happy Face cult, their motto was 'laugh through the pain.' That's what they taught Mary. Their leader used to be a stand-up comedian."

Enhart nodded. "Marshall Hanson. He was pretty incisive. But he sold out with those commercials, *'What do you want* me *to do about it?'*"

"Yeah, those were funny when I was a kid. Then he had that really preachy comeback special during the Bush Jr. presidency, acting like he was George Carlin. Everyone started calling him *brilliant*, saying he should run for president. Then he did that documentary, *Laugh Through the Pain*, about surviving his bilateral testicular cancer."

Enhart winced. "Shit, I forgot about that. Both balls."

"After that, people started calling him *inspirational*, so he made those cancer treatment centers that were part hospital, part comedy club, basically *Patch Adams* in practice, everybody laughing through the pain, putting on a happy face."

"I thought that was pretty admirable."

"It was. I guess pretty soon after that he drank his own Kool-Aid and decided he was the Second Coming of Christ."

"When he was barely the second coming of John Stewart."

"Exactly. So he built that commune out in the desert. Then a whole lot of other people started drinking his Kool-Aid, and joined him. And before it became a cult it became a sort of movement. He ran through all the talk shows, talking about his 'miracle cure-all.' Then people started *calling* it a cult, and started calling Hanson a *lunatic*, a *psychopath*, a *cult leader*. The bloom was off the rose, and that's when he started looking for people like Mary to rebrand, to improve their image. And not long after that, they all drank the Kool-Aid for real."

"You know, it wasn't actually Kool-Aid at Jonestown," Enhart said. "It's was a knockoff called Flavor Aid, laced with cyanide."

"'Drinking the Flavor Aid' doesn't have the same ring to it," Gloria said. "The Happy Face people didn't actually drink Kool-Aid either. It was Crystal Light."

Enhart shuddered. He hated the stuff with a passion, mainly because it was the only flavored drink Christie-Ann allowed in the house.

"Anyway, Mary didn't stay long with Happy Face. She left when Hanson started talking about mass suicide."

"That was unexpected, hearing about that. From

comedian to mass murderer in less than five years. Crazy stuff. And the fact that so many people went along for the ride." He shook his head somberly.

"People instinctively want to be led," Gloria said, the irony apparently lost on her. "Most of them don't even care where they're going as long as someone's taking the lead. 'The Lord is my shepherd... He makes me lie down in green pastures. He leads me beside still waters.'"

"Yeah, I guess," Enhart said. "So your friend Mary got out before the mass suicide, and *she led you* right to the Children of Dinah."

"That's right. After she left, she did a few TV interviews, especially once the Happy Facers offed themselves. Then she got into coaching. But she never felt *fulfilled*. Because gymnastics wasn't her calling. It didn't fill that hole in her heart."

"No?"

"No. That was her mother's dream for her. What she wanted was something very..." She seemed to struggle for the right word. After a moment, she settled on: "*Unique*."

"Unique how?"

Gloria smiled, almost beamed at him. "She wanted —she *needed*—to give birth to our savior."

CONFESSION

"**Y**our *savior*?" Enhart chuckled wryly, unable to believe what he'd just heard.

Gloria shook her head. "*Our* savior, Michael. All of ours."

"As in... Jesus Christ? Buddha? Mahdi?"

She sighed exasperatedly, rolling her eyes. "It's such a male-centered belief to assume the savior of humankind will be a man, or God is male. God is our creator. If God created people in *Her* image, it stands to reason She created woman first. After all, our mothers create *us*, which makes mothers our surrogates for God here on earth. That's what those Simonians were onto, I think, with their Eden/womb stuff. Have you heard of the biblical figure Lilith?" she asked, seemingly changing tack.

He nodded. "She's not mentioned in the bible, but I've heard of her, sure. Considered to be Adam's first wife according to some Jewish texts in the Middle Ages. She was banished from the Garden of Eden for disobeying her husband."

"Right. But she *wasn't* his first wife. Lilith was the first *Virgin Mother*. She *gave birth* to Adam, *and* to

Eve, making them the first virgin births. A *true miracle*, thousands of years before Mary gave birth to Jesus. The prophet of the Children of Dinah? Also a woman and a mother. So why, Michael, would you assume *our savior* would be *a man*?"

Enhart shook his head. "I guess I never thought of it that way. It does make a weird kind of sense, when you think about it. That mothers would be our models for God. What does that make fathers?"

"Fathers are doctrine," Gloria said. "Authority and discipline. Mothers are divine. Compassion. Selfless. Creative. Unconditional love."

"Not all mothers," Enhart said.

"*Mother figures*," she clarified. "That could be your grandmother, your aunt, a kindly old woman down the road. It doesn't have to be the woman who gave birth to you. Just like your father figure isn't necessarily your father at birth."

"Like you with Tracy and Bill."

"Right. Can I tell you another story? One last one?"

"Is this one of your miracles?"

"This is *all the miracles*," she said. "There was once a little boy. He was adopted, only his parents never told him that. And when he was four or five, his birth mother came and took him away from them."

Enhart leaned forward. "Is this about Mother Amelia?"

"Let me *lead*, Michael."

Enhart held back a biting response. "Go ahead, Gloria. One last story."

"This boy," she said—

He grew up on a beautiful farm, with all sorts of people like his mother, in the religious community she belonged to. They were happy people for the most part, but they were also devout, and they all worshipped a man they believed to be a prophet of God. The next *messiah*.

But like the Bible says, "Beware of false prophets, who come to you in sheep's clothing, but inwardly they are ravenous wolves."

This so-called messiah was a man like that. He had some interesting ideas, like a lot of them seem to, but he was basically a phony. Fucking all the women who were the right age to fuck, just waiting on the young girls to come of age so he could fuck them too. He preyed on the insecurities of these people. Their weaknesses. Their guilt. Told his followers they'd been wronged by society, that the world was sick, and together they'd build a utopian society of their own, free from evil, and judgment and wickedness. He was so convincing, he was able to get the men to let him sleep with their wives and daughters, because God wanted him to sire a "divine lineage" who would "survive the coming storm."

They were a doomsday cult, in other words, led by a man who thought of himself as the Second Coming of Jesus Christ. He believed the world would end when a "dangerous, charismatic leader" came into the White House, a man who'd use "Christian values" as a tool to gain political power. Well, Jimmy Carter sure wasn't that president, but when Reagan won the election in 1980, their leader started to believe the apocalypse was on the express route to Washington, DC.

The boy's mother didn't believe in any of this. She loved their leader, but not like the others did. She'd learned from him, like you said. One of their core rituals was burning their pain in effigy, something he called "sin-burning." They'd write down their biggest sins, their regrets, their traumas, the names of their enemies and the transgressions that were inflicted upon them. They'd fold these little notes up and throw them into a great big bonfire. They did this at the end of every week. She liked that part of it, because she'd had plenty to burn, and eventually, the guilt of her past sins—whether they were justified or not—she was able to burn it all away.

And she loved their leader, she truly did, but he'd changed as his power grew. She'd been there since the beginning, started it with him, but she knew nobody would believe in a female messiah. Not even in the 1970s.

Yes, technically, there was Mother Ann of the Shakers and the "holy mistress" Eve Frank in the 1700s. But those are two exceptions to the rule. Historically, messianic figures have all been men. Even Eve Frank was the successor of her father, who started the Frankist cult.

So the boy's mother, she learned from the leader, but she also taught him what *she'd* learned, and together they built a religion around his small following, until it grew to nearly a hundred members by 1981, when they died.

But the boy's mother, she saw the bad days coming. She saw power corrupting the leader, and she knew from when she was a young girl how power was malleable. That if his power was stripped away from him—by the government, for instance, as was suggested in those letters they'd been receiving from the IRS—he'd act like a cornered rat. So when she saw the winds blowing in that direction, she planned to leave, and take her son with her. She just needed to find the right time to do it.

And then, like a divine punishment directly out of the Bible, her son disappeared in the middle of the night.

Nobody knew where he'd gone.

The mother was frantic. She felt like her heart had been torn out of her chest. Like a piece of her soul had been stolen from her. Like a limb had been severed from her body.

She was *desperate* to find him. Only, the locals didn't want anything to do with them, and they'd already had too many issues with the police to get their help either.

Not to mention, she'd taken her son back from his adoptive parents without their permission, which was technically kidnapping itself.

All she knew for certain was her son didn't run away. He wasn't the type. Too much of a mama's boy. His love for her was purer than any of the other children's love for their parents. She knew this for a fact.

He never would've left her on his own.

So, someone had to have kidnapped him.

But they couldn't put out a missing persons alert for him or the couple she'd kidnapped him from would take him back. And they couldn't just let whoever'd taken him get away with it.

So the boy's mother left in the middle of the night. And the following day, the government came to collect their taxes with force. Tear gas caught fire like at Waco and seventy-three people died when the roof collapsed on the main house.

"SEVENTY-THREE PEOPLE?" Enhart interrupted, his heart pounding. This story was too close, much too close. But she couldn't... it just wasn't *possible*. "Was Mother Amelia in the Church of the Holy Wounds?" he asked, and swallowed a hard lump.

Gloria nodded slowly.

"This isn't... I would've *known*..."

"Why would you know that, Michael?" Gloria asked. She was wearing that knowing smirk again. Enhart didn't like it. It seemed to imply she had something over him, and she'd already twisted the knife in his side once tonight.

"That same thing... it happened to me," he said slowly. Deliberately. "I was supposed to die at Holy Wounds, but my father took me away *two days* before it happened. My mother... she died with the others in the roof collapse."

"Did she?"

"Yes. She did."

"What makes you so certain she died?"

He scowled. "I've spent the last forty-four years without her, Gloria. I think I'd know if my own mother was still alive."

The smirk slipped from her lips. "What if I told you your mother *survived* Holy Wounds? Would you agree that's a miracle, Michael?"

"Miracle? It's damn near impossible. Not only that, I know the names of every single person who died at Holy Wounds, and there *was* no Amelia. No Chloe, either."

"I told you, she escaped," Gloria said. "But there was a Jane on that list, wasn't there?"

Enhart's heart stopped beating momentarily. He had to grip the armrests to keep himself upright. "That's her. That's my mother."

"Your mother's name was Jane."

"Yes."

"But Jane was her *middle* name. You didn't know that, did you?"

"No, I didn't..." He shook his head, his confusion building. "Everyone just called her Jane. Are you saying my mother's dead, or she's still alive? Her name was on that list."

"It was a mistake."

"It can't be...."

Gloria nodded again, just as slowly.

"Prove it. If she's still alive, prove it, goddammit."

She nodded toward the bedside table. "Pick up your phone."

"Don't mess with me, Gloria. I told you, I'm not playing games anymore."

"This isn't a game, Michael. Pick up the phone and press Call. *Trust* me."

Enhart studied her face. She wouldn't break. If this wasn't a game, if she was serious... was it really possible his mother was still alive? After all these years?

He snatched his phone off the table. Opened it and pressed the Call button. Christie-Ann's number came up.

"Call it," Gloria said.

Enhart shook his head dubiously and pressed the Call button again. "This is ridiculous." He held the phone up to his ear.

It rang once. Twice.

On the third ring, Christie-Ann picked it up.

Only the voice that said "*Hello, Michael,*" wasn't his wife's. It belonged to an older woman.

"Who is this?" he said cautiously.

"*You know who it is,*" the woman said. "*You've al-ways suspected it, I think. I'm your mother, Mikey.*"

Enhart hung up the phone. He placed it on the table, face down, staring at it like it was a crawling in-sect. He looked up at the painting of the father and son. Back at the phone. His head was spinning. He felt like he was going to be sick.

"Who was it?" Gloria asked, the knowing smirk now a grin.

He stood abruptly. The chair skidded back along the carpet nearly a foot. "You're fucking with me," he said, jabbing a finger toward her. "How did you people get my wife's phone?"

Gloria didn't flinch. "Ask her yourself," she said calmly.

The phone buzzed on the table.

Enhart stared at it. It couldn't be true. It wasn't his mother on the other line, even if her voice did seem recognizable, especially since it seemed as if he'd heard it very recently.

The Children of Dinah had been researching him, Gloria had said so herself. They'd probably been fol-lowing Christie-Ann for who knows how long, and stolen her cell phone while she was too concerned about Jessa to think about her purse.

Or worse, they could have *kidnapped* her.

Buzzzzzz.

But what if what Gloria said *was* true, and his mother had somehow found Christie-Ann...?

He shook his head. That wasn't possible. Jane Cerice was dead. He'd seen her name on the list of victims of the Church of the Holy Wounds roof col-lapse. His mother died forty-four years ago, the year he turned thirteen.

He'd spent his whole life trying to learn more

CVLT

about her, but everyone who'd known her had died in the siege.

The phone's buzz rang in his ears.

"Fuck," he said. "What is this? What's... what's happening here, Gloria? Did you *kidnap* her? Did you people *kidnap* my wife?"

"Answer the call, Michael."

He lunged at Gloria, grabbed her by the collar of her hemp pajama top, tearing the fabric. Her penetrating gaze didn't falter, not for a second. *"What the fuck is this, Gloria?"*

A knock at the door startled him. He turned his head to look at it. The phone continued to buzz. The knocking on the door echoed it, almost like music.

Buzzzz. Knock knock knock.

Buzzzz. Knock knock knock.

"Answer it," Gloria said, looking up at him with her chin poised defiantly above his clenched fist.

Enhart gritted his teeth, snarling down at her. He thought about choking her. Punching her. Slamming her up against the wall and forcing her to tell him what they'd done to Christie-Ann and Jessa.

Then he let her go.

She slumped against the headboard, the cuffs rattling. She was still smiling, a radiant Buddha smile. He wanted to wipe it off her smug fucking face.

Instead, he went to the door.

He glanced back when he got there. Gloria hadn't moved. The smile she wore unnerved him. Who was waiting for him on the other side of that door? A couple of large cultists with a burlap sack to put over his head and a pair of shovels to dig his grave? Would they have guns? Was his number finally up?

He peered out the peephole.

"Christie-Ann?" he said.

The phone stopped ringing.

Enhart drew the chain, turned the deadbolt and threw open the door. Christie-Ann stood under the awning. Drizzle fell just beyond it. She held baby Jessa sleeping swaddled in her arms. Both her and the baby were wet.

He ushered her into the room. "What are you doing here? Are you all right? The hospital let you take Jessa home?"

Christie-Ann just smiled.

"Is she okay? Did you *walk* here?"

Enhart pushed the door closed, prepared to get a towel from the bathroom to get them dry. Something stopped the door with a thud as he turned.

A familiar gray tennis shoe held it open.

Before Enhart could react, a hand grabbed the door and shoved it back open.

Startled, he moved to protect Christie-Ann and the baby.

Two men stepped into the doorway. Three, if you counted the man with the black bag over his head and his arms held behind his back. Enhart recognized the third man's clothing. Blood had oozed down his wrinkled throat and dried there.

It was his father, Lonnie Enhart.

"Dad, what are you—?"

The two men barged into the room, pushing his father forward. The old man staggered and fell, but the men, two brutes in the gray hemp day wear of the Children of Dinah, pulled him back up to stand.

"Don't hurt him, okay?" Enhart hadn't seen his old man in nearly five years, hadn't gone to visit him even when his aunt put the old house on the market and told him Lonnie was losing his faculties and had to be put into a home.

He hated his father, had never forgiven him since the day he'd taken him away from his mother, but he wouldn't just stand here and let these brutes beat up on an old man. Not in front of his daughter-in-law and grandchild.

"Let the old man go. He's not part of this. He didn't do anything to you."

"Didn't he?" came a woman's voice from outside. The same vaguely familiar voice he'd heard over the phone.

She stepped into the doorway, dressed in a long gray cloak made of the same fabric as Gloria's pajamas and the men's day wear. Silver locks fell over her shoulders from beneath the hood. Its shadow obscured most of her face but from what he could see of it, he figured she was at least in her seventies, possibly older.

"Hello, Michael," Mother Amelia said.

Enhart realized she and the two men and his father were dry. They hadn't come from elsewhere. They'd been here, staying here in the motel. The Children of Dinah were the "convention" who'd arrived in the school bus. After what Gloria had said about them researching him, it was almost so obvious he chided himself for not having caught it before.

"I'm the one you want," he said. "Leave my family out of it."

"Oh, Mikey," the old woman said, and the musical lilt of her voice gave her identity away without him even needing to see her face. "I can't 'leave your family out of it.' We're all family here, don't you see?"

She removed the hood. It fell at her back, revealing her face, a face he remembered from his dreams, because he'd had no photos of her. She was much older, but it was definitely her.

It wasn't Mother Amelia.

It was *his* mother.

She pouted. "I see you're still confused," she said. "Let me illuminate you, Michael. Yes, I'm your mother. Yes, I survived Holy Wounds. My birth name is Chloe Jane Cerise, and on my confirmation, I was given the name of Saint Amalberga of Maubeuge, also known as Amelia."

Enhart shook his head. "No," he said, his mouth suddenly almost too dry to speak.

Because it was a miracle. An honest-to-God, hand-on-heart *miracle*.

"Yes, Michael," she said. "I'm Mother Amelia. But I'm also your mother."

CONVERSION

"When you were thirteen," Mother Amelia said, "Lonnie Enhart, your adoptive father, kidnapped you from the compound of the Church of the Holy Wounds two nights before the siege, and *one* night before I was going to leave with you. He *took* you from me, Michael. *My son*. The boy I gave birth to at the Sisters of Poor Clare convent in Des Moines."

"No," Enhart said again. It seemed to be the only thing he *could* say.

"I spent ages trying to find you. I searched all over the country. And when I finally found you, you and the man who'd taken you from me were doing the same to others that he'd done to you. Kidnapping people from their found families, shattering their beliefs, stealing their joy. You'd become like my enemy. But I knew that you could change.

"I watched you from afar. Watched you grow and learn, and become a very different man from the man who called you his son. There's *good* in you, Michael. I know that. Despite what you've done, I know you aren't like him. I see you fighting it. Your dual nature. You can still *change*."

"No," he said again.

"Yes, Michael. Don't you see? Your whole life is a lie. Christie-Ann, your wife, *she's one of us*. Or Mary, I should say." She smiled, gesturing toward Christie-Ann, who stepped out from behind Enhart and joined her at the door.

"No."

"*Yes*. I sent her to you. To be with you. She wanted to have a child, and what better child to have than the granddaughter of her prophet? Your sweet, delicate Jessa, she was born to the Children of Dinah. She'll lead us, when she's old enough. She was *born* to be *our savior*."

A tear tracked down his cheek. "Please," he said, reaching out to Christie-Ann, to Jessa. Christie-Ann —Mary, whatever her name was—took a single step back from him, closer to Mother Amelia.

It hit him suddenly. *Christie-Ann. Christian*. How had he not noticed that before? He'd been blinded by her beauty at first, and then by love. She could have called herself Mary Magdalene or Jesus H. Christ and he would've ignored it.

Jessa, he thought. *It wasn't her mother's name. It means "God exists." It's the girl version of Jesus. No wonder Christie-Ann was so insistent. She's a fucking nut. A cultist. A fucking Child of Dinah.*

"I don't understand," he said. "Bunches... it's not true. Tell me it's not true."

Christie-Ann only hugged their daughter closer to her and shook her lightly, cooing softly.

"It's true," Mother Amelia said. "All of it is true. This whole 'deprogramming,' it was all just a ruse to get you here with us. To *test* you. To see if you are worthy. A quite clever plan, too, Gloria. You were right about that."

Gloria smiled.

"What do you think? Is he worthy, Gloria?"

The younger woman nodded. "He failed a few tests but... I think so. I think we could convert him."

Her leader smiled. "Good," she said.

"But Gloria's mother," Enhart said, still not quite getting it. "She wanted me to *help* her."

"That was *me*, Michael." Mother Amelia pitched her voice up. "Please, save my daughter, Mr. Enhart. Save my poor, sweet Savannah from those cultist *freaks*."

Enhart's legs gave out. He fell backward, landing hard on the edge of the bed.

"You Enharts are *thieves* of divinity," Mother Amelia, *his* mother, said as she approached him on the bed. He smelled her perfume as she neared him, the wild roses of his youth. "But you can still atone for your sins, Michael. My poor, deluded Mikey."

"You're not my mother," he said, lying to himself.

"Oh?" Mother Amelia tugged down the left arm of her cloak, revealing the withered, faded tattoo of a pair of lips there, and the pucker of scar beneath it. The scar caused by Paul Petrichor's bullet all those years ago.

His chest hitched. Tears fell. "Mom?"

She nodded, smiling softly.

"What do I do? What do you want me to do?" he all but whimpered.

His mother removed a knife from the pouch in the front of her cloak. She held it out to him. "You have to murder him, Mikey. You have to slay your demon."

Enhart blinked. "M-murder?"

"He's not even your *real* father, Michael. Your real father is a dead priest. Or a dead exorcist. I'm not sure,

165

to be honest, and it doesn't really matter, anyway. *What matters* is you're *my son*. Your daughter is going to lead us. And you can be with us, all of us. Or you can die a sad, lonely old man like Lonnie Enhart."

"I can't... I *won't*..."

Gloria unlocked the handcuff holding her to the bed and crawled over to him. She laid a hand on his shoulder. He could only assume she'd gotten up to get the keys from his coat when he'd been out of the room that first time, answering Christie-Ann's— *Mary's*—call.

"Don't be stupid, Michael," Gloria said. "This is everything you've always wanted. A wife. A child. A *family*. Come live with us on the commune. Accept your true purpose."

Several more people entered the room behind the men holding his father, each wearing the same gray hemp day wear of the Children of Dinah. All smiling beatifically. Welcomingly. At peace. One of them was Trudy Beaumont, aka Sonny. He held the hand of Cher, aka Lucy Trillio.

They were alive. They'd been with the Children of Dinah the whole time, though he hadn't seen them when he'd done his reconnaissance.

His mother returning, Sonny and Cher alive, Jessa perfectly healthy. They weren't *miracles*. They were all just another part of the trick.

Abracadabra.

"*Join us, Michael*," everyone said in unison.

Mother Amelia held out her empty hand to him. "Mikey. This is *your life*. This is *your destiny*. All these years, you've been stealing this peace, this divinity, from others because *Lonnie* stole it from you." She offered the old man a sidelong glance full of venom. "Because if you couldn't have it, no one should. Well, *now you can.* The life you lost when you were twelve, the mother you lost, the family... it can all be yours again."

Enhart's eyes blurred with tears. He blinked them away, felt them spill down his cheeks. She was right, of course. He'd loathed his father and his father's work but over the years he'd learned to love this job they'd shared. When he was younger his motives had been selfish, like she'd said. He'd discovered a sort of malicious glee in seeing the people they'd deprogrammed together reject their personal belief and messiahs, converted by his father's often brutal, Spanish Inquisition tactics. But as he'd grown older, as he'd learned to live without his mother, without his assumed family, with only the old man to keep him company in one cheap motel room after another, he'd eventually found virtue in it. He'd discovered *purpose*. He was *helping* people.

Had he been lying to himself the whole time?

He thought about holes. When he finally learned to love this job, he thought he'd filled the hole his mother's death had left in him. When he met Christie-Ann, he realized that hole had only been poorly plastered over. And when he thought Jessa might die in surgery, he realized the plaster hadn't entirely covered the hole. It'd already started peeling back, cracking, and the child he worried he wasn't prepared to raise had actually filled it back in.

Did it matter if Mary only loved him because he was the son of her prophet? If she loved him, and they loved their child, and their child grew up in a loving, caring community—what difference should it make that it was all based on a lie?

"But there's a price," Mother Amelia said.

And here it was: the difference.

"That price *must* be paid, if you want to come with us. Slay your demon, Michael. Rise above your past. Kill Lonnie Enhart. Become the man you were always meant to be. The son of a *prophet*. The father of the *Messiah*."

Father. Son. Her words jogged loose a memory from back when this all started, when he'd first brought Gloria into the room. It didn't make any difference at all, was just another example of everything falling into place. Still, it broke the spell.

"You swapped out that painting, didn't you?" he asked, wiping away his tears.

Mother Amelia gave him a confused look. "Painting?" she said.

"Above the bed." He nodded toward it. "With the father and son on the farm."

She frowned. "We didn't do anything with the painting, Michael. This is the first time any of us have been in this room." She looked back at the others. They all nodded in unison. Gloria leaned amiably on his shoulder and nodded herself.

Enhart shrugged her arms off of him and got to his feet. "No. This is fucked. This is *fucked*, do you hear me?" He pointed at them. At *all* of them. "You people are insane. You're all... you're fucking murderers! I'm not gonna be any part of this... this *sickness*! Come on, Christie-Ann," he said, and held out his hand to her and the baby.

Christie-Ann hugged Jessa closer to her, turning slightly away from him. Denying him as Peter denied Jesus. His heart stung at the rejection.

"They don't belong to you, Mikey," Mother Amelia said. "But you *can* have them, if you follow our way."

He looked at his father, the old man's entire body

trembling under the hood. "*No*," he said again, even though this wasn't his real father. Lonnie was his adoptive father. His real father was one of two child rapists and his mother was a serial murderer and leader of a fucking death-cult.

"This is *madness*, don't you see?" He directed it to all of them, but was only met with blank looks.

Finally, his mother, *their* mother, drew the knife away from his reach. "He's not *ready*," she said, a sickened look on her face. "He's not *one of us*."

"*No*," all the voices boomed at once, even Gloria's, still on the bed, like she'd always been.

"He'll *never* be one of us."

"*Never*," they all said.

"But the price must still be paid. Vengeance *must* be enacted." She nodded at the others.

The men holding his father—the only father he'd ever known—pulled the hood off the old man's head. Lonnie Enhart looked terrible. His eyes were bloodshot, yellowed and cloudy with cataracts. His cheeks were sallow, and the skin—bristly with stubby silver hairs—hung loose from his jowls. He'd aged twenty years in the past five, and Enhart felt himself pitying the man, despite everything his father had done to him over the years. He'd taken Enhart back from his mother, his *real* mother, because he'd loved him, in his own way, even if that love was sometimes harsh. Why else would he have spent so much time looking for him? Why else would he have raised his adopted son to be like him?

Lonnie looked around himself. Frightened. Confused. Enhart wondered if he even knew what was happening. His aunt had said the old man was going senile the last time they'd talked. If he was lucky, he didn't even know he was about to die.

His eyes fell on Enhart. Enhart saw recognition bloom there.

"S-son?" his father said, confused but no longer scared.

"Dad," Enhart said, his eyes tearing up again. Two men stepped out of the group and grabbed him by the arms before he could intervene. Gloria leaped off the bed and laughed wickedly, *impishly*, at his side.

In the next moment, Mother Amelia stabbed his father in the gut. The old man doubled over with a moan, hanging from the hands of his captors, his bleary eyes widening, his lips peeling back from tombstone gray teeth in a horrified grimace.

"Dad!" Enhart cried, struggling against the men who held his arms behind his back.

Lonnie Enhart's eyes glazed over and he slumped forward, the life leaving him.

"Dad!" Enhart cried again. He turned to his father's murderer. "How could you do that? He was just a sick old man, you sadistic bitch!"

His mother wiped the blade clean on a gray handkerchief. "What did we do with a sick animal at Holy Wounds, Michael? We put it out of its misery. Take him away," she said, nodding to the men holding his dead father.

The crowd parted and the two men trundled out, marching the old man out of the room, the toes of his loafers dragging on the reddish-orange carpet.

Enhart's lower lip quivered as the tears streamed down his cheek. He couldn't believe what was happening. His whole life, stripped from him in a matter of minutes. His wife and child, cultists. His mother, a psychotic cult leader. His adoptive father, murdered. His birth father, a long-dead rapist. He couldn't possibly imagine a worse fate befalling anyone.

He felt like Job from the bible. He half expected to turn into a pillar of salt, like Lot's wife as they left the town of Sodom.

"You are *not* my son," Mother Amelia said, and somehow this was the harshest blow of them all. She tucked the blade back into the pocket of her cloak and nodded to her followers, and the men and women of the Children of Dinah began marching out of the room, following the men who carried his father.

Gloria looked back at him with an evil leer as she followed the others into the gray, drizzly morning. Christie-Ann favored him with a look of pity. At least there was no malice in her departure, even though she took with her the only child he was likely to ever have.

And Enhart pitied her, because she didn't know what she was doing, *couldn't possibly* know what she was doing. She'd been brainwashed, like the rest of them. Swayed by this wolf in sheep's clothing who called herself his mother, and theirs.

At last, he was left alone with the old woman herself. Even the men who'd held him had let him go and left with the others, disappeared into the chilly autumn morning.

"That's it?" he asked, rubbing his wrist, sore from one of the men wrenching it back. "You're just gonna let me walk away?"

The old woman cocked her head. "It's like Gloria said, isn't it? If someone takes your eye, take the eyes of their family, their friends. But you leave *them their* eyes to *witness it*." She let the words hang for a long moment, studying him. "We'll be seeing you, Mikey."

Enhart watched her leave. He thought about telling her he'd involve the police. Shouting after her that she wouldn't get away with it, that he'd tell the Feds and they'd raid her compound and the same

171

thing he'd thought had happened to her all those years ago would happen for real this time.

Only he still cared for Christie-Ann, despite her betrayal. It was complicated, but what love didn't have its complications? And he loved the daughter they'd made together. He couldn't let what happened to the Church of the Holy Wounds happen to them. Or what happened in Waco.

One day, when she was old enough to travel but still too young to remember it, he'd slip into their compound in the dead of night and take Jessa back from these people.

Until then, he'd always be looking over his shoulder, worried they'd come back for him.

Because no matter what Mother Amelia or Gloria had said about leaving him his eyes, to them he was still just another man of Shechem.

And if the Children of Dinah knew anything, it was *revenge*.

ACKNOWLEDGMENTS

As always, I need to thank a few people. No book is written entirely without others. There are always first readers, editors, proofreaders, etc. This book is no exception.

I always thank my ever-patient wife, Sherri, for being my *first* first reader, but this time around I need to thank her for pushing me to write this at all. I gave her the opening chapter to read when I was trying to decide what to write after finishing *Helloween*, and she insisted I write this one. This book literally wouldn't exist without her. Whether that's good or not I'll leave for you to decide.

Also need to thank my mom, Carol, who was staying with us at the time I was writing this and was surprised at how quickly this story poured out of me. (I'd been sitting on the concept and vague outline for at least 7 years, so it was less of a surprise to me. Alas, 7 years ago I don't think I could have written it as well.)

Thanks also to my good friend Danika Meyerson, who had conversations with me about this book a long while ago when neither of us knew what these conversations would lead to. She truly *gets* it.

Extra thanks to beta readers Andrew Adams (author of *Son of a Serial Killer*) and Amber Corbin for their valuable input and catching more errors than I could have without their eyes.

That's all for now. I truly hope you dug this entry into the Lonely Motel series. I've got at least two more books in the works for it (including the swan song entry for Shyla and Angel), and I'm super excited for what's to come. I hope you'll continue on this journey with me. Your room is waiting....

D.R.
August, 2025

ABOUT THE AUTHOR

Author of the cult smash-hit *Woom* and *Ghostland* and more than 15 other books that aren't the cult smash-hit *Woom* or *Ghostland*. His debut collection was blurbed positively by the legendary Jack Ketchum. His vampire novel, *Pedo Island Bloodbath*, was nominated for a 2024 Splatterpunk Award for Best Novel, and his ghost technothriller, *Ghostland*, is soon to be a board game from Crystal Lake Publishing and co-creator Jon Cohn (author of *Kill Beth* and *Slashtag*).

For 10 *free* dark fiction short stories/novellas including the prequel to *GHOSTLAND*, "The Moving House," signed copies of Woom, bookplates and merch, please visit www.duncanralston.com.

For more delicious dark fiction,

visit **www.duncanralston.com**

and **www.shadowworkpublishing.com.**